What God Expects of MEN

What God Expects of MEN

Bill George

All Scripture quotations, unless otherwise indicated, are taken from the *Holy Bible: New International Version®*. *NIV®*. Copyright © 1973, 1978, 1984 by International Bible Society. Used by permission of Zondervan Publishing House. All rights reserved.

Scripture quotations marked *NKJV* are from the *New King James Version*. Copyright © 1979, 1980, 1982, 1990, 1995, Thomas Nelson, Inc., Publishers.

Scripture quotations marked KJV are from the King James Version of the Bible.

This book is a revision of a work published originally under the title *What God Expects of Me*.

Pathway Press is pleased to donate a special copy of *What God Expects of Men* in support of this special cause. Because we believe in the spiritual development and building up of strong individuals of faith for the kingdom of God, Pathway is pleased to be a part of this endeavor. May this book inspire, teach, train, and effectively touch your life in a positive way.

Kenneth T. Harvell, General Director of Publications

Library of Congress Catalog Card Number: 97-67556

ISBN: 871489260

Copyright © 1997 by Pathway Press

Cleveland, Tennessee 37311

This book is dedicated
with appreciation to

Leonard C. Albert

A gifted colleague,
a faithful friend,
a leader of men.

CONTENTS

INTRODUCTION

Genesis, the first book of the Bible, is a study of how everything got started. The first few chapters tell how God created the world and everything in it. The narrative describes how that last of all, He created man.

God's first conversation with Adam, the first man, was something like a training session. God told him what he could eat and what he couldn't eat. He showed him where he would live, and He let Adam know what He wanted him to do.

As a new Christian you have a lot in common with the first man. Spiritually speaking, you live in a new world. Jesus used the expression "new birth" to describe what happens when a person gets saved. Paul, the man inspired by the Holy Spirit to write much of the New Testament, used similar words when he wrote: "Therefore, if anyone is in Christ, he is a new creation; the old has gone, the new has come!" (2 Corinthians 5:17).

The study of this book will help you find out what God expects of you. Just as God explained to Adam some do's and don'ts and gave him work to do, God also has instructions for you as well as tasks for you to perform.

This book is based on the Bible. As you use this book, you will notice that it contains many references to passages in the Bible. You will find your studying much more enjoyable and beneficial if you will take time to look up these scriptures and read what they say. The scriptures in the text of this book are taken from the *New International Version* of the Bible. You may wish to use it or the *New King James Version* for your studies. Or you may prefer the time-honored King James Version.

At the end of each chapter you will find the words "FOR FURTHER STUDY." The books listed in this section contain helpful information about the subject you have studied in the chapter. You may wish to buy these books for your personal library. Most of them are available through the Church of God Publishing House. Write Pathway Press, 1080 Montgomery Ave., Cleveland, TN 37311; or call toll free: 1-800-553-8506.

When you have completed the study of this book, you should have a clear idea of what God expects of you as a Christian man.

–1–

What Really Happened
When I Got Saved?

⭐ Why do people need to be saved in the first place?

⭐ What does the word *saved* really mean?

⭐ How does a revolutionary change take place in a person's life?

This book deals with these questions plus scores of others like them. The purpose of this work is to help you to understand what it means to become a Christian. A careful study will enable you to better explain to others what happened when Christ came into your heart. People use certain terms to describe their conversion experience and sometimes the terminology is confusing. Some of the key words you will understand better when you have finished this chapter are . . .

- Redemption

- Justification

- Reconciliation

- Regeneration.

These terms are used to describe the process and results of what we commonly call "getting saved." The Bible gives good advice in 1 Peter 3:15: "Always be prepared to give an answer to everyone who asks you to give the reason for the hope that you have." This chapter will help prepare you.

What Causes the Change?

A junior in college began attending church. After a few weeks he responded to the pastor's invitation to give his life to the Lord Jesus Christ. His experience naturally caused some changes in his way of thinking, talking, and acting. It was no surprise to him when, after a couple of weeks, one of his old friends, noting the changes, asked, "What in the world has happened to you?"

God expects Christians to understand, to a certain degree, what has happened to them in the experience that is called "getting saved," "conversion," or "giving your heart to the Lord."

Redemption—I'm Redeemed

A hymn we sing uses the expression "I'm redeemed!" A good starting point for understanding what has happened to you is this very word—*redeemed*. It is used commonly in conversations about pawnshops. Suppose a person who owns an expensive watch discovers he needs money. He takes his watch to a pawnshop. The pawnbroker accepts the watch and gives the man a certain amount of money for it. Along with the money, the pawnbroker also gives him a "redemption ticket." The customer may return with the ticket, the amount of money he received from the broker for his watch, plus extra money for interest—and buy back his watch. He can "redeem" his watch.

Basically, this is what has happened in the life of a person who has become a Christian. Man originally belonged to God. Because God created him and loved him, man was related to God—much as a child is related to his father. Instead of obeying God, however, man chose to turn away from Him and live according to his own desires and wishes. Man chose not to belong to God. As a matter of fact, we can think of man as a rebel against God.

Man's choices were bad; they were in conflict with God's will. Man's bad choices are called sin. They separate him from God and make him guilty and deserving of punishment. The situation was further complicated because man is unable to pay the price required to make up for his sins. In the opinion of God, only a perfect man could possibly make up for the badness of all men. God, in His love and mercy, provided Someone who could pay the price for man's sin. God gave His only Son, Jesus Christ, who came to earth and lived as a man. Jesus died, even though He was guilty of nothing bad, so that His death could make amends for the sins of all men (and women, boys, and girls).

Do you remember how you felt when you grasped the fact that you were guilty of having sinned and that you were a sinner in the eyes of God? How terrible it was to realize that within yourself you had no power to do anything to help yourself! You were hopelessly lost! Then it dawned on you that Jesus Christ had paid the price that you could not pay! You decided that with His help you would turn away from the sin that separated you from God. When you trusted in Him and what He did on your behalf, then you were saved.

Meaningful words are used in the church to describe what happens. One of these words is *redeemed*, which we have already discussed. When we talk about Christ's redeeming us, we mean that He is the One who paid the price for our sin so that we could once again belong to God. This is what Christ said of His own ministry in Mark 10:45: "For even the Son of Man did not come to be served, but to serve, and to give his life as a ransom for many."

Atonement—I'm Right With God

Perhaps you have heard sermons which urged the hearers to "get right with God." The Bible uses a beautiful word to express what it means to be right in the eyes of God. It appears often in the Old Testament, but only once in the New Testament (KJV). It is the word *atonement*.

By looking closely at this word, you will see that it is made up of three smaller words: *at-one-ment*.

Think back to what we looked at earlier. God wants humanity to live in harmony with Him and to enjoy fellowship with Him. But God's holy nature cannot tolerate the presence of sin. Sin has come between God and man, and has caused separation.

The good news, according to Romans 5:11, is that "we also joy in God through our Lord Jesus Christ, by whom we have now received the atonement" (KJV). When you were saved, you received "at-one-ment." That is to say, you were no longer separated from the presence of God; you were "at one" with Him. Do you remember what a good feeling it was when you realized that you were no longer separated from God?

"We . . . joy," the verse says. This means we have reason to be happy. And happiness extends into heaven itself. Luke 15:10 tells us, "There is rejoicing in the presence of the angels of God over one sinner who repents."

Peace—I'm at Peace With God

Along with the feelings of joy and happiness that you have experienced comes a deeper emotion which we call peace. *Peace* means "freedom from strife; harmony and concord; an undisturbed state of mind." Paul explains it simply: "We have peace with God through our Lord Jesus Christ" (Romans 5:1).

A vivid word picture of this peace is found in another book of the Bible. In Ephesians 2, Paul discusses the relationship that existed between Jews and non-Jews during the lifetime of Christ. He pointed out that in the Jewish temple there was a barrier, a wall beyond which Gentiles could not go. They could not enter the inner recesses of the Temple, the area reserved for the Jewish people. Paul thought of this wall as a symbol of the division that exists between men and other men, as well as between men and God. So he said, "For he himself is our peace, who has made the two one and has destroyed the barrier, the dividing wall of hostility" (v. 14).

What Christ did when He paid the price for your sin was to literally break down the dividing barrier that existed between you and God. When neighbors quarrel and cannot get along, they build a fence to prevent access and fellowship. How different it is when the neighbors are loving, close friends who experience constant, happy togetherness! There is no fence!

You have peace when you are saved. There is no fence between you and God!

Justification—The Judge Says, "Not Guilty!"

What has happened to the sins you have committed that were on your record? According to the Bible, the record is clear; you no longer have to answer for those sins.

The word we use to describe this happy state of affairs

is *justification*. Paul used this term often. The word comes from the Roman-law courts and may be illustrated by a man being brought to court to answer for a crime. Then, for some reason, he does not have to stand trial; he is acquitted. Simply, he is *justified*.

The Word of God says that as a Christian you are justified in the presence of God. Because of what Christ has done, you don't have to go on trial for your sins. Quite literally, *justification* means "just as if I'd never sinned."

Another good way of thinking of justification is to compare it with forgiveness. The two concepts are basically the same. The difference is that *justification* is more of a legal term, whereas *forgiveness* is a more common and personal concept. For example, you use the legal term (*justification*) when you are thinking in terms of an accused person being acquitted by a judge; you use the more intimate term (*forgiveness*) when you think about pardon being extended by a person who has been offended.

You will find a good discussion of justification in Romans 3:23-26. These verses explain that all men have sinned and come short of what God expects. They need an uprightness which they are incapable of producing. But God, through Christ, produces it for them.

On March 5, 1994, Deputy Sheriff Lloyd Prescott was teaching a class for police officers in the Salt Lake City Library. As he stepped into the hall, he quickly took note of a man with a gun forcing a large group of men and women into a room a few doors away. Without thinking, Prescott, who wasn't in uniform at the time, joined the group. Once inside, the gunman announced that he had taken the group hostage and would begin executing them one at a time. The deputy immediately identified himself as a policeman and, in the confusion that followed, fatally shot the man in self-defense. The people who had been held captive were released safe and unharmed.

As Officer Prescott did for captive people that day, so Jesus Christ has released us from an even greater bondage. Entering our world dressed in street clothes, He moved among men who had been taken hostage by Satan; and, on the cross, He defeated the Enemy and set the captives free.

Since you have accepted Christ as your Savior, you'll never have to stand before Him when He is judging men to decide if they belong in the kingdom of heaven. In His eyes, you are already declared innocent and set free!

Reconciliation—We're No Longer Enemies

Have you ever started to discuss a mutual friend's divorce action, only to be told, "Oh, haven't you heard the good news? They have reconciled their differences; they're not getting a divorce."

You know what is meant by that. Whatever the problem was that had caused the separation has now been resolved. It has been dealt with and settled and is no longer a factor that will result in divorce.

Reconcile is one of the Bible words that explains what has happened to you. In its other form, *reconciliation*, it means "a renewal of friendship." Those who before were enemies and who had differences that hindered their friendship have resolved those problems and are now friends once more.

The opposite of *reconcile* is *alienate*. People who cannot, or will not, get along with each other are *alienated*. But those who have resolved their difficulties and now enjoy the company of one another are *reconciled*.

Before you were saved, you were alienated from God. Paul describes such people in Ephesians 4:18: "They are darkened in their understanding and separated from the life of God because of the ignorance that is in them due to the hardening of their hearts." He explains reconciliation in Colossians 1:21, 22: "Once you were alienated from God and were enemies in your minds because of your evil behavior. But now he has reconciled you. . . ."

What this means in a nutshell is that you are no longer an enemy of God; you are His good friend!

I Can Call Him Father

If someone were to ask you what is the clearest picture in the Bible of a sinner who returns to God and is accepted by Him, what would you answer? No doubt you would probably think of the story of the Prodigal Son (Luke 15).

A son asks for his inheritance before his father dies, runs away and wastes all the money. Finally, he returns home broke, hungry, and destitute. His father, whom we might have expected to turn him away, welcomes him home and treats him with love, dignity, and respect.

This story wonderfully illustrates the eagerness with which God pardons a repentant sinner who returns to Him. It also teaches another equally meaningful lesson: the intimate Father-son relationship that exists between God and His spiritual children.

One of the words the Bible uses to describe this close relationship is *adoption.* Adoption is a word familiar to most of us today because of the common practice of adopting children. Prospective parents happily welcome a new child into their home and enter into a parent-child relationship just as if the child had been born to them.

The key Scripture passage that explores this idea is Romans 8:15: "For you did not receive a spirit that makes you a slave again to fear, but you received the Spirit of sonship. And by him we cry, 'Abba, Father.'" *Abba* was an affectionate way of saying "Father" in the language spoken in Palestine in Paul's day. It is similar to the expression "Daddy" that we use today.

It means a lot to say you've been adopted into the family of God. When you think about all the implications of being able to call God "Father," you realize just how great it is! Perhaps most amazing of all is that, according to the Bible, when we become His children we also become "heirs of God and co-heirs with Christ" (v. 17).

Regeneration—I've Been Changed

Perhaps the greatest happiness of your Christian experience will come from the certain knowledge that you've been changed. Think about how the Bible pictures the difference in your old life and your new life.

You have been born again. You have been born from above. You are a new creation. You have become pure in heart. You are forgiven. You have been made alive. You are a new man. All these expressions signal change.

The change takes place by *regeneration.* It might be helpful to think of regeneration as the divine side of what we call *conversion.* It is a work of God. We can even say it is a miracle of God. By an act of His favor, He changes the disposition of the soul so that it is renewed in the image of Christ. The sin you once enjoyed now seems awful to you, and you no longer want to engage in it. Sin no longer dominates your life as it once did. Instead, Christ occupies the center of your life.

A recent Christian convert—one who had been regenerated by the power of God—heard a Sunday school teacher talking about the greatness of the miracle of Christ's turning the water into wine in John 2. "I can tell you of a greater miracle than that," he responded, "which God performed in my own life. In my case, Christ turned wine into furniture, a car, and clothes for my children!" What he was saying, of course, was that the regenerating power of God was stronger than his love for alcohol and had empowered him to defeat the awful hold it had on his life. Now he could use his earnings to properly care for his family.

You have been changed! It wasn't the result of turning over a new leaf; it was the result of turning over a life! It didn't come because of your own wishing and willing; it came because of His great power and on account of His great love. *Regeneration* is just a longer word for what we call the "new birth."

In one of the early Rose Bowl games, in 1929, Georgia Tech and UCLA were pitted against each other. In the first half, a young California player named Roy Riegels recovered a UCLA fumble, but in the excitement he ran 65 yards the wrong way! A teammate ran him down and tackled him just before he scored for Tech. His error made it possible for the Georgia team to score a safety a couple of plays later.

At halftime, Riegels sat alone in a corner of the locker room. Almost nothing was said by the coach or any player. Just before the second half was to begin, the coach announced that the same players that had started the first half would start the second. When the other players started out of the room, Riegels remained still in the corner. The coach called him, but the embarrassed young man told him, "Coach, I can't go back out there. I've failed you, the university, and myself!" The coach placed his hand on his shoulder and said, "Roy, get up and get out there. The game is only half over!"

The young player finally got up, returned to the field, and played one of his best games ever.

You may be among those who have been running the wrong way for a long time. But because of what Jesus Christ has done, the game is not yet over. You are forgiven! You can start over! You are changed!

And There's More!

These are just a few of the ways the Bible talks about the wonderful experience that has occurred in your life. As you study further in this book, you will learn much more.

The important truth to grasp is that you are *saved*! *Saved* is the opposite of *lost*; and "lost" described your condition before you were found by Christ. Unhappily, we cannot agree with those people who say that everyone in the world is a child of God and that God is the Father of all. In the sense that He created us, this is true. But the Bible speaks too clearly of the awful consequences of sin and the separation caused by sin, as well as of the redemptive suffering of Christ, for us to treat it lightly or to think of His suffering and death as unnecessary.

You can now sing with all the saints of God the praise hymn that will be sung to Christ in heaven:

> With your blood you purchased men for God from every tribe and language and people and nation. You have made them to be a kingdom and priests to serve our God, and they will reign on the earth (Revelation 5:9, 10).

You can join in the old hymn of the church that says:

> Blessed assurance, Jesus is mine!
> Oh, what a foretaste of glory divine!
> Heir of salvation, purchase of God,
> Born of His Spirit, washed in His blood.
> This is my story, this is my song,
> Praising my Saviour all the day long!
>
> —Fanny Crosby

THE CHAPTER REVISITED

"A changed life" is perhaps the best description of what it means to be saved. In this chapter you explored the dimensions of religious conversion. In the process you discovered the meaning of familiar Biblical and theological words that are used to describe the changes that take place in an individual's life when he comes to know Jesus Christ as his Savior.

As a result of learning this material, you will be more ready to "give a defense to everyone who asks you a reason for the hope that is in you" (1 Peter 3:15, *NKJV*).

FOR FURTHER STUDY

Little, Paul. *Know What You Believe*. Wheaton, Ill.: Scripture Press Publications, Inc., 1987.

Packer, J.I. *Growing in Christ*. Wheaton, Ill.: Crossway Books, 1994.

Stott, John R.W. *Basic Christianity*. Downers Grove, Ill.: InterVarsity Press, 1977.

—2—

He Expects Me to Be Sure

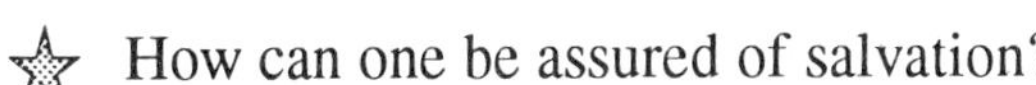

⭐ How can one be assured of salvation?

⭐ How can I have the bold spiritual confidence
I so admire in others?

This important issue is the focus of our study in this chapter. Knowing what God's Word has to say to us on the subject, and believing His Word, will give you a glorious assurance of your salvation.

Suppose someone had approached you a few moments after your dramatic saving encounter with Jesus Christ and asked, "Are you saved?" Most likely your reply would have been, "Oh yes, I'm saved! I feel wonderful!"

That's descriptive, but it's not a good-enough answer.

A Christian cannot base the assurance of his salvation solely on the level of his feelings. It is quite likely that a new convert will sense contentment and joy upon realizing that he has peace with God and the gift of eternal life. But it is equally probable that his newfound happiness will eventually wane and that somewhere along the way, it will be replaced by depression.

Human emotions are notoriously unreliable. Someone has compared feelings, or emotions, to a roller coaster— soaring to the heights of elation, then plummeting to the depths of despair. Doctors say that certain mood changes can result from improper diet. The lack of certain food elements in one's body may cause temporary feelings of depression. It is certainly foolish, then, to let emotions control your sense of spiritual well-being.

If you can't trust your feelings, how can you ever know for sure that you are saved? A brief study of what the Bible has to say about the security of the believer will help you. Many Christians say that they have been strengthened at this point by a consideration of the Book of 1 John.

John explained to first-century Christians, and to us, why he wrote the epistle: "I write these things to you who believe in the name of the Son of God so that you may know that you have eternal life" (5:13). He had been one of the 12 disciples of Jesus and he stressed the idea that Christians can know certain spiritual truths without doubt. The word *know* (or a similar form of the word) appears more than 30 times in the brief Book of 1 John. The Holy Spirit can also speak to you and help you to find assurance of your salvation through the words He inspired 20 centuries ago.

Believing His Word

John said:

We accept man's testimony, but God's testimony is greater because it is the testimony of God, which he has given about his Son. Anyone who believes in the Son of God has this testimony in his heart. Anyone who does not believe God has made him out to be a liar, because he has not believed the testimony God has given about his Son (1 John 5:9, 10).

This means that what God says is greater than what men think or say. God has laid down certain basic truths in His Word. A few of these are listed here. You would do well to commit these basic scriptures to memory.

Christ received you. "All that the Father gives me will come to me, and whoever comes to me I will never drive away" (John 6:37).

Christ holds you always and won't turn loose. "I give them eternal life, and they shall never perish; no one can snatch them out of my hand" (John 10:28).

Christ will never abandon you. "God has said, 'Never will I leave you; never will I forsake you.' So we say with confidence, 'The Lord is my helper; I will not be afraid. What can man do to me?'" (Hebrews 13:5, 6).

Christ forgives you when you sin and He cleanses you. "If we confess our sins, he is faithful and just and will forgive us our sins and purify us from all unrighteousness" (1 John 1:9).

You won't be tempted more than you can bear. "No temptation has seized you except what is common to man. And God is faithful; he will not let you be tempted beyond what you can bear. But when you are tempted, he will also provide a way out so that you can stand up under it" (1 Corinthians 10:13).

All of these Scripture verses are facts. No doubt there will come a time when you won't "feel" saved. You may even begin to doubt whether you ever really exercised faith. When these experiences occur, pull out these verses and tell God, the devil, and everybody else that this is God's Word and you are going to stand on it!

Keeping His Commandments

Basing your experience on the facts of God's Word is the surest way to know that you are saved. But it is not the only way. John says, "We know that we have come to know him if we obey his commands" (1 John 2:3).

Jesus evidently placed great importance on His followers' obeying His commandments. When He was talking to His disciples on the night before He was crucified, He told them that He was not going to refer to them as servants anymore, but as friends. Then He added, "You are my friends if you do what I command" (John 15:14).

This business of obeying Christ makes sense. He has come to the earth to set up His kingdom. Anytime people live together, there is a need for rules and standards to govern conduct. If we lived in a world where everyone obeyed God's will, it would be an ideal world—without crime, poverty, war, or any of the factors that mar human relationships. Someday, when we get to heaven, we will live in that kind of world. In the meantime, the Lord wants us to be models of the kind of citizens who will inhabit His kingdom.

What does that have to do with knowing you are saved? When you are born again, your new nature wants to live His kind of life. There is something within you that urges you to make the right choices. It checks you when you make a wrong choice. John puts it this way: "We know that we have come to know him if we obey his commands" (1 John 2:3).

Deeply agitated and upset, a young man approached his pastor. "I am afraid the devil has me in his power and I am no longer a child of God," he cried. Then he explained that he had slipped back to an old habit which had plagued him before he became a Christian.

The pastor talked with him long enough to realize that it was a momentary lapse and the young man was deeply sorry and sincerely repentant. "Look," the pastor counseled, "the very fact that you are here weeping and confessing to Christ is the best sign that the devil does not control your life." Together they prayed and thanked God for the desire that the young man had to serve God and to live a holy life.

When you have the spirit of Christ in your life, you don't want to do wrong constantly. Instead, you are driven to repentant prayer when you realize that you have displeased your Lord. This desire to keep His commands is one of the ways you know you are saved.

Loving the Brethren

John mentions another proof of our salvation in the following observation:

> If anyone has material possessions and sees his brother in need but has no pity on him, how can the love of God be in him? Dear children, let us not love with words or tongue but with actions and in truth. This then is how we know that we belong to the truth, and how we set our hearts at rest in his presence whenever our hearts condemn us (1 John 3:17-20).

An urgent desire in our hearts to put our love for others into action is a signal that we belong to Christ. Christ gave the world the greatest demonstration of love it has ever known.

This kind of love is characterized by a willingness to "lay down our lives." There is much more involved than an easy-come, easy-go, "be-nice-to-everyone" kind of charity. This kind of love is characterized by a willingness to sacrifice personal good for the benefit of another—an altogether rare and unnatural quality in today's dog-eat-dog, what's-in-it-for-me kind of world.

If you sense impulses to go out of your way for the well-being of someone else, it's an encouraging indication that certainly Christ is at work in your life. This kind of effort is not without its reward. Jesus told His friends that when they obeyed His commands and went out of their way to minister to others, it was as though they had done it personally to Him (see Matthew 25:40).

Receiving the Spirit

One of the more satisfying assurances of your salvation will be the fact that the Holy Spirit lives in you. In 1 John 4:13, John puts it this way: "We know that we live in him and he in us, because he has given us of his Spirit."

The Bible teaches that your salvation is a work of the Spirit: He performs the new birth; He testifies of Christ in your life. The Christians in the New Testament set a pattern in their experience, however, which lets us know that a constant fullness may be added to the indwelling of the Spirit. After He has done His work of redemption, the Holy Spirit will come to the believer in an empowering baptism to equip him for service. If you are a Christian, if you are obeying your Lord, and if you fervently desire His presence in your life, you may receive this baptism of power. The fact of His arrival and His ministry in your life will be a constant reminder that, indeed, you are a child of God.

A college student approached his final exam in a logic class with a professor who was known for his impossible examinations. The professor explained that each student would be allowed to bring as much help to the exam as would fit on a piece of notebook paper. On the day of the test, most students brought an 8½ x 11 sheet of paper crammed with everything they could write in the space. This particular student, however, placed an empty sheet of notebook paper on the floor beside his desk and had a doctoral student in logic, a friend of his, stand on the paper. The advanced student told him the answer to every question on the exam and he was the only test taker to receive an "A."

You, too, will face a final examination when the God of heaven asks you, "Why should I let you in?" By yourself you can never pass that test. Thank God for Someone who will stand at your side and speak for you at that moment!

You can be sure!

THE CHAPTER REVISITED

Being a Christian is a matter of right belief, right behavior, and conscientious day-by-day practice. Someone has observed that it is a matter of head, heart, and hands.

In this chapter you learned that you may be assured of your salvation by . . .

- what Scripture tells you about it

- your willingness to follow the commands of Christ

- your interaction with other believers

- the internal witness of the Holy Spirit, who now lives inside you.

One thing for sure: Don't trust your capricious feelings! Instead, believe God. He has a lot of experience in keeping people saved.

FOR FURTHER STUDY

Marshall, I. Howard. *Pocket Guide to Christian Beliefs.* Downers Grove, Ill.: InterVarsity Press, 1991.

Rhea, Homer. *A New Creation.* Cleveland, Tenn.: Pathway Press, 1996.

—3—

He Expects Me to Confront Temptation Successfully

★ Why do things like this suddenly appear in my life?

★ Why me, Lord?

★ What happens if I fail in temptation?

These are some of the most frequently asked questions of Christians. It seems that you barely entered into your new life when you begin to be tempted to turn back to the world and its ways. The purpose of this lesson is to help you learn how to successfully deal with temptation. The key word is *temptation.*

Together we will explore the reality of temptation as it is taught in Scripture. The Word of God will help you understand why and how temptation comes to you. More importantly, a study of this chapter will help you to know how to overcome temptation and come out victoriously.

Everyone Is Tempted

The first idea that crossed your mind after you were saved might have been, "Thank God! Now that I've given my heart to the Lord, I am through with sin." It probably didn't take you long to discover how mistaken was that notion. As a matter of fact, it is quite likely that you now notice temptations to sin even more than before you were converted.

Everyone is tempted to sin. Simon Peter, who was one of the original Twelve and later a leader in the church, wrote to his fellow believers: "Dear friends, do not be surprised at the painful trial you are suffering, as though something strange were happening to you" (1 Peter 4:12). He was saying to them—and to you—that temptation is inevitable and is to be expected.

The business of Satan is to tempt God's people. He began his work in the Garden of Eden by deceiving Eve, and he has been successfully tempting people ever since.

The first step you should take in dealing with temptation, then, is to acknowledge that it is going to come. As surely as day follows night, as surely as winter comes after autumn, temptation will follow your encounter with God. It was true in the experience of Jesus himself. One of the most powerful spiritual occurrences of His life was His baptism, when the Spirit descended in the form of a dove and the Father spoke aloud to His Son. But what happened immediately afterward? The Bible says, "Then Jesus was led by the Spirit into the desert to be tempted by the devil" (Matthew 4:1).

What Temptation Is

Let's be sure at the outset that we are talking about the same thing when we use the word *temptation.*

Temptation is an incitement of natural desires to go beyond the bounds that God has set. Almost always, temptation has to do with normal, natural desires and inclinations which are God-given and not sinful when gratified as God intended.

The Bible doesn't catalog sins in clear categories, but one verse in particular suggests different aspects of sin. In 1 John 2:16 we read, "For everything in the world—the cravings of sinful man, the lust of his eyes and the boasting of what he has and does—comes not from the Father but from the world." What this verse means is that when you indulge yourself, strive to obtain things and do things outside of God's desire for you, then it is sin. It is the mission of Satan, the tempter, to incite you to give in to wrong desires or to try to gratify natural desires in wrong ways.

Help! I'm Being Tempted!

If you overcome temptation successfully, you have to resist it. In James 4:7, you have the God-given assurance: "Resist the devil, and he will flee from you." The Bible pictures the devil as a roaring lion, prowling around and looking for someone to devour (1 Peter 5:8); but in the same passage believers are told to resist him (v. 9). Would God tell you to do something that is impossible to do?

To give you even more confidence in the matter, Paul teaches:

> No temptation has seized you except what is common to man. And God is faithful; he will not let you be tempted beyond what you can bear. But when you are tempted, he will also provide a way out so that you can stand up under it (1 Corinthians 10:13).

Be honest enough to admit that if you really want to sin, you are going to go ahead and do it. It's only when you want to live a holy life that you will resist temptation. Your identification with Christ, then, lies at the heart of victory over sin. If He lives in you, you will not want to do anything contrary to His will. If you find yourself doubting, slipping, unsure, leaning toward un-Christlike desires, it's a signal to turn to Him for strength and guidance. We'll study more along this line in succeeding chapters.

At times you may be uncertain about whether a course of action is sinful or not. What does one do in such a case?

God's Word doesn't give lists of what is sin and what is not, although it does make clear certain sinful practices. It also spells out principles that you can apply. It would be a good habit to ask yourself certain questions when you are confronted with temptation:

- Will this action bring glory to God?

- If Jesus were in my place, would He do it?

- Can I ask God to bless me in doing it?

- Will this action hurt or offend anyone?

- Would I want to be found doing this when Christ returns?

The answers that the Holy Spirit brings to your mind will help you to decide the right course of action.

Getting Ready to Face the Devil

If temptation is a sure thing in the life of a Christian . . . if Christians should indeed resist the devil . . . if Christians sometimes feel they are unable to handle temptation on their own—how can they prepare themselves for the battle? Again, the Bible gives instructions and examples for guidance.

Your primary weapon against the devil is the strength and power of the Word of God.

"How can a young man keep his way pure?" asks the psalmist; and he immediately answers his question: "By living according to your [God's] word" (Psalm 119:9).

Then, in verse 11 he adds, "I have hidden your word in my heart that I might not sin against you." Someone once wrote in the front of his Bible, "Sin will keep you from this Book, but this Book will keep you from sin."

Again we turn to the example of Jesus. The devil came to Him with three temptations. Interestingly, these three temptations fall into the three classes mentioned in 1 John 2:16—the temptation to indulge oneself (lust of the flesh), the temptation to obtain things (lust of the eyes), and the temptation to do things in ways other than God's way (pride of life). In all three cases, Jesus' reply and rebuke to the devil was, "It is written" (Matthew 4:4, 7, 10). Jesus used the written Word of God to overcome the devil. You can do the same!

Consider this revealing information about Jesus: "For we do not have a high priest who is unable to sympathize with our weaknesses, but we have one who has been tempted in every way, just as we are—yet was without sin" (Hebrews 4:15). We must suppose that the pattern Jesus set in winning over temptation in the wilderness—quoting the Bible to get rid of the tempter—was the method He used when He was tempted "in every way, just as we are." We can wield the sword of the Spirit, which is the Word of God, just as Jesus did, and we can win the victory over the devil.

Another thing you can do is stay out of places where you might reasonably expect to confront temptation.

The old *Hee Haw* television show once showed an episode

where a patient entered the office of Dr. Campbell and complained that he had broken his arm in two places.

"Well, then," declared the country doctor, "you better stay out of them places!"

You cannot regularly place yourself in places where you expect to be tempted and not be affected. You need to take Dr. Campbell's advice: "Stay out of them places!"

The Spirit's Role

You may find it somewhat confusing to read that temptation is a work of the devil and then encounter statements that God, or the Spirit of God, has something to do with it. How can we reconcile this apparent contradiction?

It is certain that all experiences and circumstances in the life of a Christian are under the control of the Father. The apostle Paul told about a trying circumstance in his life (see 2 Corinthians 12) in which he referred to a "thorn in the flesh," which he described as a "messenger of Satan." He ascribed his temptation to the devil. Yet, he recognized that God had the power to take away the thorn. While we must understand that no prompting to sin comes from God, we must also understand at the same time that God sometimes permits such trials in order to accomplish His own purposes.

God sends us trials to make us better; the Enemy sends us temptations to destroy us. James gives us this example:

Consider it pure joy, my brothers, whenever you face trials of many kinds, because you know that the testing of your faith develops perseverance.

Perseverance must finish its work so that you may be mature and complete, not lacking anything. . . . Blessed is the man who perseveres under trial, because when he has stood the test, he will receive the crown of life that God has promised to those who love him (1:2-4, 12).

God may permit the devil to tempt you, but rest assured that He will never allow you to be tempted beyond your capacity to endure and overcome. Using the Word of God as a spiritual weapon, you can defeat the devil.

And If I Fail . . . ?

What happens if, despite all your efforts to resist, you fall into sin? Run quickly back to Jesus! The powerful message of 1 John 1:9 is, "If we confess our sins, he is faithful and just and will forgive us our sins, and purify us from all unrighteousness." First John 2:1, 2 explains that God doesn't want us involved in sinning; but if we ever do sin, we have an Advocate, Christ Jesus, who will plead our case in God's presence.

THE CHAPTER REVISITED

Successfully dealing with temptation is the theme of this chapter.

Some men who have a saving experience with Christ want to throw up their hands and quit when they are tempted, thinking that something must be wrong with them. As a matter of fact, temptation is common to all men.

Your reaction to temptation will be to resist it because you are helped and strengthened by the presence of Christ in your life. As your High Priest, He is constantly praying for your deliverance from evil.

What happens if you fail in temptation? Run back to Jesus and admit your failure. He will readily pardon you, cleanse your life, and help you get on your feet again. He wants you to have victory even more than you do!

FOR FURTHER STUDY

Anderson, Neil. *The Bondage Breaker*. Eugene, Ore.: Harvest House Publishers, 1992.

— 4 —

He Expects Me to Know His Word

⭐ How should I think of the Bible?

⭐ Why should I study it?

⭐ What is the best way to study God's Word?

A father bought his 4-year-old son a Christmas present. He chose a little pedal car which came unassembled with all the parts packed in a box. On Christmas Eve, after the boy was asleep, the father began to put the car together. Much to his dismay, he discovered the manufacturer had packed the wrong instructions with the car. The company, which produced other wheeled items, had mistakenly included directions for assembling a baby carriage instead of the pedal car. What should have taken only 30 minutes developed into a four-hour project, because he had to work without directions.

The Bible is God's instruction book. In it you will find directions for living your Christian life. The key words you will study in this chapter are . . .

- Scripture

- Covenant.

Our purpose is to better understand the relationship of the believer to the Word of God. We will suggest why and how you can use the Bible to achieve a balanced, happy Christian life.

How Should I Think of the Bible?

Looking at it objectively, the Bible is a collection of 66 books and letters, written by about 40 authors over a span of perhaps 16 centuries. It contains poetry, history, biography, sermons, and predictions of future events.

But the Bible is more. It is the Word of God. Man is able to understand many things by science and reason, but the best way he can learn things about God is for God to reveal them to him. The Bible contains God's revelation of Himself.

The Bible, then, is a very special book. No other book has the weight of authority that the Bible has. It is divinely inspired; that is, the human authors who penned the words of the Bible were guided by God as they wrote. This means that the message of the Book is a message from God. Peter put it this way: "For prophecy never had its origin in the will of man, but men spoke from God as they were carried along by the Holy Spirit" (2 Peter 1:21). Paul wrote: "All Scripture is God-breathed and is useful for teaching, rebuking, correcting and training in righteousness, so that the man of God may be thoroughly equipped for every good work" (2 Timothy 3:16).

The majesty of the Bible, its great length, and the awe that it inspires have caused some new Christians to fear to open it for study. Your reaction should be just the opposite! God has revealed truths about Himself, about man, about sin, about creation, and about many other subjects. He revealed these truths precisely because He wants us to learn them.

Incidentally, it will be helpful if you realize that the Bible can be read in a relatively short time. While a serious course of Bible study will take longer, it has been proven that the average reader can read from Genesis to Revelation in about 80 hours.

It Looks So Complex!

The person who opens the Scriptures for the first time is confronted with an index page that lists columns of strange-sounding names. Divided into two sections, the first and longer column is called the Old Testament, and the shorter column which follows is called the New Testament. *Testament* means "covenant"—or, as we would say today, "agreement." The Old Testament is the account of people who lived under an old type of agreement with God, and the New Testament tells about God's new agreement with mankind through Jesus Christ.

The names of the 66 books seem somewhat strange because they come from forms of languages that no longer exist. The Old Testament was written mostly in Hebrew with a few passages in Aramaic. The New Testament writers used Greek. (Modern Hebrew and Greek languages are different from the forms used to write the Bible.)

Open your Bible to the index page and let us look at the list of books.

Old Testament

The first five—Genesis, Exodus, Leviticus, Numbers, and Deuteronomy—are called the Books of the Law. They are called this because a large part of their content is the law of God as given to Moses—including, for example, the Ten Commandments. These books begin with the story of Creation and continue until the death of Moses. Fascinating stories are told about such persons as Adam, Noah, Abraham, Isaac, Jacob, Joseph, and Moses.

The 12 books which follow (Joshua through Esther) are traditionally referred to as the Historical Books. They are called this because they record the history of the Jewish people.

Job, Psalms, Proverbs, Ecclesiastes, and the Song of

Solomon are categorized as the Poetic Books or Wisdom Literature.

The remaining 17 books in the Old Testament, the Prophetic Books, record the sermons and messages of prophets. The first five are referred to as the Major Prophets, and the other 12 are called the Minor Prophets. This does not reflect on the importance of their work, but only the relative length of their writings.

New Testament

The New Testament contains four Gospels, one history book, 21 letters, and one prophecy book.

The Gospels—Matthew, Mark, Luke, and John—relate facts about the life and teachings of Christ. Acts is a history book that catalogs some of the story of the church from about A.D. 30 to A.D. 60. Of the 21 Epistles (this word means "letters"), at least 13 (perhaps 14) were written by the apostle Paul. Seven (or eight) were composed by other church leaders. These letters were originally written to churches and individuals to give them guidance, instruction, and encouragement.

The last book, the Revelation, is dedicated principally to predictions of events to take place in the future.

Why Should I Study the Bible?

You ought to study the Bible because in it God reveals Himself and His will to you. From its pages you can draw strength and help. The Book itself explains that it is like food that nourishes the body: "Like newborn babies, crave pure spiritual milk, so that by it you may grow up in your salvation" (1 Peter 2:2).

The Bible also has a cleansing effect upon the life of a Christian. "Sanctify them by the truth," Jesus prayed for His followers, and then He added, "Your word is truth" (John 17:17). The Word hidden in your heart will keep you from sinning, according to Psalm 119:11.

The Bible is your soulwinning tool. Your own arguments carry no authority, but His Word is backed up with power. According to Hebrews 4:12, it is "living and active. Sharper than any double-edged sword, it penetrates even to dividing soul and spirit, joints and marrow; it judges the thoughts and attitudes of the heart."

How Can I Study?

Dozens of books available in Christian bookstores offer counsel and suggestions for different methods of Bible study. Many students say that it is helpful for them to first use a regular dictionary to look up words that they don't know, then use a Bible dictionary to learn more about people and places that are mentioned in their reading.

The following ideas are important if you wish to gain the greatest benefit from reading the Bible:

1. *Read the Bible daily.* Just as your body needs regular

meals in order to stay strong, you also need the Word of God to remain spiritually healthy.

2. *Pray before you read.* Ask the Holy Spirit to open your mind and to help you to understand what God wants to say to you.

3. *Read in a pattern.* That is, don't just let the Book fall open and begin reading. Select a book of the Bible and read it through on successive days.

4. *Start with easier parts of the Bible first.* Many readers find that Mark or John is a good beginning place. The Psalms are also helpful and not difficult to read.

5. *Use a good version.* There are dozens of versions of the Bible. Some are translations, and some are paraphrases. A translation is produced directly from Hebrew and Greek manuscripts and attempts to convey exactly what the text says. A paraphrase, on the other hand, attempts to say basically the same thing, but in language arranged for ease of understanding. The most widely accepted version of the Bible is the King James Version, translated in 1611. Readers discover that the meanings of some words have changed and that the style of the King James is not exactly the way we talk today. For beauty and majesty of language, however, the King James Version is unsurpassed and is a trustworthy, reliable translation. A good recent translation is the *New International Version*, which is used in this book. Other good ones are the *New King James Version* and the *New Living Translation*. Some versions have been translated by people who do not believe the Bible to be inspired; therefore,

changes have sometimes been made that alter the meaning. Ask someone who is familiar with the versions before you purchase one.

6. *Look for a personal message in your reading.* That is, ask yourself, "What does God want to say to me in this passage?"

7. *Keep a notebook.* When you discover a truth that is meaningful for you, write it down.

8. *Read with a plan.* With the help of a mature friend, decide on a course of study that will take you through the whole Bible, book by book.

The Bible: Book of Books

An unknown writer has left us with the following testimony of what the Bible is to every believer:

> Someone describes packing his bag for a journey. Before closing it, he observes a small corner not yet filled. He says, "Into this little corner I will put a guidebook, a lamp, a mirror, a microscope, a telescope, a volume of choice poems, several well-written biographies, a package of old letters, a book of songs, a sharp sword, and a small library of more than 60 volumes." Yet, strange enough to say, all these did not occupy a space more than three inches long by two inches wide.

> "But how could you do it?"

> "Well, it was all in the packing—I put in my Bible."

THE CHAPTER REVISITED

No other book in the world is like the Bible. It is the only book that God has given in order to reveal Himself. Many other books are helpful, but the Bible was written by men who received the thoughts and inspiration for writing them directly from the Author of Life.

This chapter has given you background about the organization and layout of the Bible, and has made suggestions about how you can get the most out of it in your studies. Don't be put off by what appears to be the "complexity" of the Bible. It is from God. He has gone to great lengths to preserve it down through the centuries; and He wants you to know what it says. Read it. Study it. Learn it. Enjoy it. Benefit from it.

FOR FURTHER STUDY

Arthur, Kay. *How to Study Your Bible.* Eugene, Ore.: Harvest House Publishers, 1994.

Mars, Henrietta C. *What the Bible Is All About.* Glendale, Calif.: Regal Books, 1987.

—5—

He Expects Me to Communicate
With Him

★   Why should I pray?

★   How should I pray?

This chapter explores the subject of prayer. Our purpose is to learn about the importance and the benefits of prayer. The Bible has a great deal to say about the importance of staying in touch with the Father. You will be strengthened and you will grow spiritually as your prayer life deepens and matures.

It is altogether amazing that the Creator of the universe has issued a standing invitation to every believer to come into His presence at will, but this is exactly the case. The inspired writer of Hebrews says, "Let us then approach the throne of grace with confidence, so that we may receive mercy and find grace to help us in our time of need" (4:16). The means by which we communicate with God is prayer.

The key scripture for this chapter is Matthew 6:9-13.

The Bible outlines the conditions under which God hears and answers prayer. It also records fantastic examples of the results of prayer.

Why Prayer?

Have you ever wondered why God created man in the first place? The Bible never gives an outright answer to that question. Among other reasons, however, it seems that God receives pleasure from man's company and communion. While Adam and Eve remained in the Garden of Eden (Genesis 1—3), they seemed to have enjoyed regular periods of fellowship with their Creator. Prayer is the method by which we enter into the presence of God, praising Him and petitioning Him.

The prophets, psalmists, and Jesus himself often encouraged God's people to pray. Among the enjoinders to prayer are these scriptures:

- "Look to the Lord and his strength; seek his face always" (1 Chronicles 16:11).

- "O you [God] who hear prayer, to you all men will come" (Psalm 65:2).

- "Ask and it will be given to you; seek and you

will find; knock and the door will be opened to you" (Matthew 7:7).

- "Then Jesus told his disciples a parable to show them that they should always pray and not give up" (Luke 18:1).

- "Until now you have not asked for anything in my name. Ask and you will receive, and your joy will be complete" (John 16:24).

These verses and many others let us know that God is interested in our prayers, and they furnish sufficient encouragement for us to dedicate time and effort to praying.

Benefits of Prayer

Prayer ensures certain benefits to the child of God.

Prayer delivers from trouble. "'Because he loves me,' says the Lord, 'I will rescue him; I will protect him, for he acknowledges my name. He will call upon me, and I will answer him; I will be with him in trouble, I will deliver him and honor him'" (Psalm 91:14, 15).

A foreigner making his first Alpine climb in Switzerland was flanked by two experienced guides. It was a dangerous ascent, but he felt secure with a guide in front and another behind as they plodded upward for hours. At last they neared the summit.

The guide in front wanted the young climber to reach the top first, so he moved aside to allow him to go ahead.

Not realizing the danger of the storm-strengthened gales that blew on the summit, the young man started to rise. The lead guide dragged him back with a stern warning: "No! Stay on your knees! You are never safe here except on your knees!"

Prayer delivers from temptation. "Watch and pray so that you will not fall into temptation. The spirit is willing, but the body is weak" (Matthew 26:41).

Prayer brings joy to the believer. "Ask and you will receive, and your joy will be complete" (John 16:24).

Prayer supplies needs. "The poor and needy search for water, but there is none; their tongues are parched with thirst. But I the Lord will answer them; I, the God of Israel, will not forsake them" (Isaiah 41:17).

Prayer provides communion with God. "I love those who love me, and those who seek me find me" (Proverbs 8:17).

These are a few of the many benefits of prayer.

George McCluskey was a man who believed in the power of prayer. Many years ago, when he first started his family, he was convicted of the need to pray daily for his children. After a while he started praying for his grandchildren and great-grandchildren, yet unborn. He prayed for their future companions and their life's work.

McCluskey's two daughters married men who entered the full-time ministry. To the two couples, four girls and a boy were born. All of the girls married preachers and the boy became a preacher. The first two children born to the next generation, both boys, attended college together. The two cousins were roommates. One answered the call to become a pastor, but the other followed his interest in psychology, eventually earning a doctorate. He is well known as Dr. James Dobson, best-selling author and host of the radio program *Focus on the Family.* Through his prayers, George McCluskey affected people far beyond his immediate environs.

Conditions of Successful Prayer

What has been your experience with prayer? Some Christians testify to almost miraculous answers to their petitions, while others say they are not sure if they can cite direct answers to any of their prayers. The Bible makes it clear that there are certain conditions under which we must pray if we are to expect positive responses to our prayers.

Faith. Jesus told His disciples, "Whatever you ask for in prayer, believe that you have received it, and it will be yours" (Mark 11:24). The opposite of faith is unbelief, and unbelief has often hindered the work of Christ. Matthew explains at one point, "And he [Jesus] did not do many miracles there because of their lack of faith" (13:58). Your attitude must be one of trust in God's power and in His willingness to answer your prayers.

Obedience. In this respect, we read these assuring words: "Dear friends, if our hearts do not condemn us, we have confidence before God and receive from him anything we ask, because we obey his commands and do what pleases him" (1 John 3:21, 22). An attitude of unwillingness to obey God's commands results in God's disapproval. An Old Testament example of this truth is found in 1 Samuel 15, which you should take time to read. Saul was rejected as king over God's people because he refused to obey God.

Righteousness. Psalm 66:18, 19 puts it rather bluntly: "If I had cherished sin in my heart, the Lord would not have listened; but God has surely listened and heard my voice in prayer." A New Testament example is equally plain: "The prayer of a righteous man is powerful and effective" (James 5:16). A man who has not rejected a sinning lifestyle cannot expect to remain in communion with a holy God.

Wholeheartedness. The testimony of Scripture is this: "You will seek me and find me when you seek me with all your heart" (Jeremiah 29:13). On the other hand, a stern warning goes out to those who treat lightly the things of God and who choose not to fear the Lord. About these, God says, "They will call to me but I will not answer; they will look for me but will not find me" (Proverbs 1:28).

Spiritual praying. There is abundant Biblical evidence that God is not impressed with long, carefully worded, elaborate, and repetitious prayers (see, for example, Matthew 6:7; 23:14, KJV). What touches the heart of God is the earnest, intense cry from the heart of His child. At times you might not understand the exact way you ought to pray. The words you need won't come. At such times, says the Bible, the Holy Spirit will pray through you and for you.

Here is the passage that explains this ministry of the Spirit: "The Spirit helps us in our weakness. We do not know what we ought to pray for, but the Spirit himself intercedes for . . . the saints in accordance with God's will" (Romans 8:26, 27).

Even though you don't know the direction you ought to go in your prayer, the indwelling Spirit of God does know, and He prays for you. In your times of prayer, yield to Him and allow Him to perform His prayer ministry through you.

A Model Prayer

Jesus' disciples were rightly concerned about prayer. They observed their Lord's habit of spending time alone with God. One day they petitioned Him, "Lord, teach us to pray" (Luke 11:1). His answer to their request was to give them a model prayer. We often refer to it as the Lord's Prayer. Let's look at the elements of this prayer which was first given to teach believers how to pray. Perhaps you can gain some insights that will help your own developing prayer life. (You can read the prayer in Matthew 6:9-13 and Luke 11:2-4.)

Our Father in heaven. The prayer begins with a recognition of the fact that a Father-child relationship exists between God and His people. This was a completely new idea in the time of Christ; it was made possible by His redeeming work. Believers can now enter into the presence of God as a child enters the presence of his earthly father.

Hallowed be your name. One of the aims of true prayer is worship and adoration. When you pray, you should spend some time at the beginning of your prayer, giving glory and honor to the Father.

Your kingdom come. Christ came to set up a Kingdom, and He has begun it by changing the lives of people so that they can be fit citizens of that Kingdom. The Kingdom will be firmly established only when Jesus returns to earth from heaven, defeats the powers of evil, and begins His earthly rule. In this part of the prayer, request that Jesus' kingdom will come soon. Always pray in the spirit of John, recorded in the closing verses of the Book of Revelation. When Jesus said, "Surely I come quickly," John responded, "Even so, come, Lord Jesus" (22:20, KJV).

Your will be done on earth as it is in heaven. Christ's will is done in heaven. We think of heaven as a place of peace, order, and perfection. Things work out right when the will of God is done. This aspect of the prayer is a request for God to have His way in the affairs of this world.

Give us today our daily bread. When you pray, you are acknowledging your dependence on a higher power. This part of the model prayer lets us know that we can depend on our Father for spiritual blessings and for material provision. It is also recognition that ultimately all we have comes from God.

Forgive us our debts. Just as bread is the basic physical necessity, so forgiveness is the basic spiritual necessity. We should always enter into God's presence with a consciousness of how far short we fall of the holiness of God. We should always approach Him with the plea on our lips that He will forgive those shortcomings. Jesus built into the model prayer the basis upon which God will forgive us—that is, our own attitude of forgiveness toward those who have wronged us. The measure that we forgive others is the measure of forgiveness that we may expect from God.

Lead us not into temptation, but deliver us from the evil one. God has the power of protecting us from the evil of this world. Jesus teaches us to depend upon the Father for deliverance from the traps and temptations of Satan.

The King James Version includes a beautiful ascription of praise to close the prayer: "For thine is the kingdom, and the power, and the glory, for ever. Amen" (Matthew 6:13).

Have you ever visited Niagara Falls? More than 500,000 tons of water plunge over the falls every minute. On March 29, 1948, however, the water trickled to a stop. What caused the flow to cease? A windstorm on Lake Erie had sent tons of ice crowding into the entrance of the Niagara River near Buffalo, effectively creating a dam. Until the ice shifted, some 30 hours later, the falls were silent. People thought it was the end of the world.

Cold indifference in the life of a believer can stop the flow of communion with God. We "should always pray and not give up" (Luke 18:1).

THE CHAPTER REVISITED

Why should men pray? Perhaps the best answer is that God enjoys it and man benefits from it. Numerous times God invites us to talk with Him. The good results are fellowship with God, deliverance from trouble and temptation, the supplying of our needs, and unfathomable joy.

The Bible spells out certain conditions that help us pray well. These include faith, obedience, righteousness, wholeheartedness, and dependence upon the Holy Spirit to help us pray.

One way to know for sure that we are praying as Jesus taught is to use The Lord's Prayer as a pattern and include in our praying the elements that Jesus employed in His model prayer.

FOR FURTHER STUDY

Arthur, Kay. *Lord, Teach Me to Pray in 28 Days.* Eugene, Ore.: Harvest House Publishers, 1995.

Blackaby, Henry. *Experiencing God.* Nashville, Tenn.: Broadman/Holman, 1994.

Bounds, E.M. *Power Through Prayer.* Grand Rapids: Baker Books, 1992.

Triplett, Bennie S. *Praying Effectively.* Cleveland, Tenn.: Pathway Press, 1990.

—6—

He Expects Me to Be
Filled With the Spirit

⭐ Is there a difference between being converted and being filled with the Spirit? If so, what is the difference?

⭐ What is the ministry of the Holy Spirit in the life of a Christian?

⭐ How does a person experience the baptism of the Holy Spirit?

The answers to these questions are vitally important to your spiritual growth, maturity, and service. Salvation is the greatest spiritual experience any person can have. Once you are saved, however, it is the will of God for you to be baptized with the Holy

69

Spirit. Learning what the Bible says about the Holy Spirit will lead you into new depths in your experience with God.

Read and study this chapter prayerfully and open your heart to what God wants to do for you. You will learn what the Bible says about the Holy Spirit, and how He empowers believers' lives today.

Converted and/or Spirit-filled

It is one thing to experience conversion; it is quite another to be filled with the Spirit.

The Holy Spirit is active in conversion; this is part of His ministry in today's world. When telling His disciples that they could expect the coming of the Spirit after He departed, Jesus explained: "When he comes, he will convict the world of guilt in regard to sin and righteousness and judgment" (John 16:8). Part of the purpose of the Spirit's coming to the world is to make men aware that they are guilty of sin and in need of a Savior. You would never have turned to Christ and placed your faith in Him if it had not been for the convicting work of the Holy Spirit.

The Spirit is the One who applies the work of redemption to your life. This takes place in the new birth. Teaching about the new birth in John 3:5-8, Jesus said that it is accomplished by the Spirit.

In His parting instructions to His disciples, the Lord told them that the Holy Spirit would comfort them, teach them, and guide them. On the evening of the day He was raised from the dead, the Bible says He breathed on them and said, "Receive the Holy Spirit" (John 20:22). Paul, reflecting on the indwelling presence of the Spirit in believers' lives, teaches us, "If anyone does not have the Spirit of Christ, he does not belong to Christ" (Romans 8:9). The Spirit is referred to at various times as "the Spirit of God," "the Spirit of Christ," "the Spirit," "my Spirit," "the Holy Spirit," and "the Holy Ghost." There is no difference in these designations; they all refer to the same Person.

It is abundantly clear that every saved person is *indwelt* by the Holy Spirit. But the Bible also teaches that it is possible to be *filled* with the Spirit, and that this filling is an experience separate and apart from being converted.

What the Bible Teaches

The disciples were saved, but they were baptized in the Spirit seven weeks after Jesus returned to heaven. A large number of people in Samaria were converted under the ministry of Philip. Then, later, when Peter and John visited them, they received the Holy Spirit. Paul had a marvelous conversion encounter on the road to Damascus; then, three days later he was filled with the Spirit. Many years elapsed between the conversion of some former disciples of John and the time they received the Spirit, but it happened. These examples from Acts 2, 8, 9, and 19 set the Biblical pattern: First, you are saved; then, subsequently (it may be in moments, days, or years) you receive the Spirit.

The Spirit's Ministry

Why is the baptism in the Holy Spirit provided for believers? The Scriptures teach us about certain ministries that He fulfills in our lives.

1. *The Spirit empowers for service.* "But you will receive power when the Holy Spirit comes on you; and you will be my witnesses in Jerusalem, and in all Judea and Samaria, and to the ends of the earth" (Acts 1:8). Christ's disciples, who had just spent three years in the company of the Lord, were instructed not to preach one sermon, testify to one person, or sing one hymn until they were filled with the Spirit. If they needed the presence of the Spirit in their lives, how much more do we need Him today!

2. *The Spirit guides and directs.* On various occasions, according to the Bible, the Holy Spirit gave directions to the church and to individual Christians. Consider these examples:

- "'We gave you strict orders not to teach in this name,' [the high priest] said. 'Yet you have filled Jerusalem with your teaching and are determined to make us guilty of this man's blood.' Peter and the other apostles replied: 'We must obey God rather than men!'" (Acts 5:28, 29).

- "While they were worshiping the Lord and fasting, the Holy Spirit said, 'Set apart for me Barnabas and Saul for the work to which I have called them'" (Acts 13:2).

- "Paul and his companions traveled throughout the region of Phrygia and Galatia, having been kept by the Holy Spirit from preaching the word in the province of Asia" (Acts 16:6).

This is in fulfillment of Christ's words in John 16:13: "But when he, the Spirit of truth, comes, he will guide you into all truth. He will not speak on his own; he will speak only what he hears, and he will tell you what is yet to come."

3. *The Spirit teaches.* Another promise shared by Jesus, which relates to this aspect of the work of the Spirit, says, "But the Counselor, the Holy Spirit, whom the Father will send in my name, will teach you all things and will remind you of everything I have said to you" (John 14:26). This means that our spiritual eyes are opened so we can see divine truths. It means that, with this reliable Teacher filling our being, we can grasp with greater clarity the significance of what the Bible says. How many times Christians have testified that in moments of despair or great need, the Spirit has brought to their minds passages of Scripture that spoke directly to their situation!

4. *The Spirit prays.* In the lesson on prayer (chapter 5) we learned that at times we don't understand how we ought to pray. At such times, the Spirit within literally prays for us: "In the same way, the Spirit helps us in our weakness. We do not know what we ought to pray for, but the Spirit himself intercedes for us with groans that words cannot express. And he who searches our hearts knows the mind

of the Spirit, because the Spirit intercedes for the saints in accordance with God's will" (Romans 8:26, 27).

Are you mechanically or technologically inclined? What would you do if the copier in the office broke down? Most employees would be unable to repair it. Even if they called the copier store, they would probably be unable to describe specifically what was wrong because they would not know the names of the parts or what was at fault.

In those cases, the copier company sends out a technician. While working on the copier he is able to call back to the shop and name the parts that need replacing. He is in a position to communicate to the maker what is needed for repairs to be made, because he knows the vocabulary. Romans 8 tells us that the Holy Spirit does this for us. When we don't know how to pray, the Holy Spirit knows exactly what we need and communicates it to the Father in a language that is completely understandable!

5. *The Spirit gives gifts.* To ensure the success and effectiveness of the church, God has promised that its members will be given special capabilities. These special capabilities are of divine origin, and the Bible calls them spiritual gifts. There are a number of these gifts. Part of the ministry of the Spirit is to distribute these gifts among the members of the church (see 1 Corinthians 12).

6. *The Spirit helps.* The Holy Spirit is called *Helper* (*NKJV*), *Counselor* (*NIV*), and *Comforter* and *Advocate* (*KJV*). These words are translated from the Greek word *Paraclete.* No one word is capable of conveying the exact

meaning of Paraclete. It literally means "one who comes alongside to help." The Holy Spirit comes to help. If the help needed is comfort, He comforts. If the help needed is direction, He directs. If the help needed is intercession, He intercedes. Whatever you (as a child of God) need, He comes to help you. Praise God for this ministry of the Spirit!

According to a recent newspaper story, a Los Angeles motorcycle policeman saw an early-morning driver run a stop sign. He turned on his emergency light and pursued the fast-traveling pickup truck, not realizing that the driver was fleeing the scene of a convenience store robbery. The driver, spotting the flashing lights behind him, pulled over.

As the policeman walked up to the truck to ask for identification, the frightened robber pointed his pistol point blank at the officer's chest and pulled the trigger. The impact knocked the policeman to the pavement. What happened next completely stunned the shooter. The policeman stood up, pulling his gun at the same time, and fired two shots at the truck. One bullet broke a window glass, the other penetrated the door and struck the robber in the leg. Screaming for mercy, the driver threw his pistol and the bag of money he had taken from the store out the window.

What he did not know was that the policeman was wearing a bulletproof vest made of Kevlar. Less than a half-inch thick, it had protected its wearer from the bullet fired just inches away.

The Holy Spirit comes alongside to help us in ways that we recognize and in ways that we may never know.

How to Receive

So far, we have established that (1) the baptism of the Holy Spirit is a spiritual experience which comes after conversion and (2) the Holy Spirit performs vitally important and unique ministries in the life of a Christian. What remains to be discovered is how to receive this Baptism. The Bible gives us the following information:

1. *He fills clean lives.* The primary requirement for receiving the baptism of the Holy Spirit is that your life be changed by the new birth and cleansed by the sanctifying power of Christ. In foretelling the coming of the Spirit, Jesus said, "The world cannot accept him, because it neither sees him nor knows him" (John 14:17). In all the cases in the New Testament, the individuals who were baptized in the Spirit first responded to the gospel with saving faith; they then received the Spirit.

Underlining this idea, Paul teaches: "Do you not know that your body is a temple of the Holy Spirit, who is in you, whom you have received from God? You are not your own; you were bought at a price" (1 Corinthians 6:19, 20).

2. *He fills those who desire Him.* The Holy Spirit does not come uninvited or unwanted. While it is the Father's great desire to equip all His children and to be present in

their lives through His Spirit, yet He waits until His presence is sought; He never intrudes.

Jesus taught His followers: "If you then, though you are evil, know how to give good gifts to your children, how much more will your Father in heaven give the Holy Spirit to those who ask him!" (Luke 11:13). This seems to be an extension of the blessing He pronounced during the Sermon on the Mount when He said: "Blessed are those who hunger and thirst for righteousness, for they will be filled" (Matthew 5:6). The Spirit baptizes those who fervently seek His presence in their lives.

3. *He fills obedient Christians.* In defending his preaching of the gospel before a Jewish court, Simon Peter—who was Spirit-baptized on the Day of Pentecost—injected a little-noticed statement: "We are witnesses of these things, and so is the Holy Spirit, whom God has given to those who obey him" (Acts 5:32). Obedience, said Peter, is one of the characteristics of the person who desires to receive the Spirit. Peter also implied that God does not pour out His Spirit indiscriminately. He gives the Holy Spirit only to those who obey God. Obeying Christ, in simplest terms, means doing what He said.

4. *He fills those who have faith.* "He redeemed us in order that . . . by faith we might receive the promise of the Spirit" (Galatians 3:14). Faith is another prerequisite for the infilling of the Spirit. This implies a simple acceptance of His promises. Some people try to "earn" the Spirit by good works, by spiritual exercises, by making bargains

with God. All He asks, however, is that you meet the conditions of a sanctified life, be hungry for His presence, and be obedient to His will; then, as you accept His Spirit just as you accepted salvation—which was by faith—He will fill you.

The Evidence

No study of the Spirit would be complete without a consideration of the evidence that the Baptism has occurred. Although there are numerous evidences, including a more active witnessing experience and great joy, the first evidence, according to the Bible, is speaking in tongues.

This was a normative New Testament experience. In every case where a person or group received the baptism of the Spirit, the Bible either clearly says or strongly implies that the evidence of the infilling was speaking in tongues. Thousands of individuals in today's Christian community who have experienced the same witness testify to its truth.

The scope of this study does not allow an in-depth investigation of speaking in tongues; however, two of the books listed under "For Further Study" will help you explore this Biblical truth.

THE CHAPTER REVISITED

The person and work of the Holy Spirit has been a much-neglected subject during many years of church history, but it was newly discovered in the 20th century. Beginning around the turn of the century with the Pentecostal Movement and receiving fresh vigor in midcentury with the advent of the Charismatic Movement, the doctrine of the Holy Spirit has once again come into the forefront of the experience of God's people. According to David Barrett in *World Christian Encyclopedia,* the Pentecostal-Charismatic family of churches is now among the largest in Christendom.

Chapter 6 spells out the differences in our understanding of being converted and being Spirit-baptized. It establishes, by using Scripture, the fact that receiving the Holy Spirit baptism is an experience subsequent to salvation. The Holy Spirit is sent to fill the lives of believers to empower them for sharing their faith, to furnish guidance and direction, to teach, to intercede, to give gifts, and to help in other ways.

How does a person receive the Holy Spirit? He meets the conditions laid down by God: a redeemed life, a spiritual hunger, obedience, and faith.

FOR FURTHER STUDY

Black, Daniel. *A Layman's Guide to the Holy Spirit.* Cleveland, Tenn.: Pathway Press, 1988.

Horton, Stanley. *What the Bible Says About the Holy Spirit.* Springfield, Mo.: Gospel Publishing House, 1995.

Hughes, Ray H. *Who Is the Holy Ghost?* Cleveland, Tenn.: Pathway Press, 1992.

Lowery, T.L. *The Baptism of the Holy Ghost.* Washington, D.C.: Lowrey Ministries International, n.d.

−7−

He Expects Me to Know
and to Do His Will

★ How does one know what the will of God is for his
life?

★ What steps does one follow to discover God's will?

These and similar questions will be examined in this lesson. Our purpose is to guide you in a Biblical and personal study about the will of God, and furnish you with information about knowing and doing His will. The key verse is Colossians 1:9.

The entrance to the harbor at Green Turtle Bay in the Bahamas appears to be broad and open. But experienced boatmen know that beneath the tranquil surface lie dangerous rocks. Only a narrow channel gives access to safe

81

anchorage. Pilots find the entrance by lining up two buoys which have been strategically placed in relation to a marker on shore. When all three objects are in a straight line, the boat is directly in the channel entrance.

God has made arrangements whereby you can know and do His will. Certain signs will let you know what He wants you to do in your Christian life and service.

God Has a Will for You

A 19th-century American minister preached a sermon about the will of God in which he said, "God has a definite life-plan for every human person, guiding him, visibly or invisibly, for some exact purpose in life, which it will be the true significance and glory of his life to have accomplished." He used Emperor Cyrus as an example, a man who, according to the prophet Isaiah, was to be the ruler responsible for the return of the people of God from Babylonian Captivity. God said: "I will raise up Cyrus in my righteousness: I will make all his ways straight. He will rebuild my city and set my exiles free" (Isaiah 45:13; see also vv. 2, 14). Isaiah prophesied *long years before Cyrus' birth,* indicating what God's will would be for this man.

This is one of dozens of Biblical examples of individuals whose lives were chosen by God to accomplish a meaningful purpose. Abraham was set apart to be the father of the Hebrew nation. Joseph told his brothers who had sold him into slavery: "You meant it for evil, but God meant it for good" (see Genesis 50:20). Moses was raised up to deliver the Israelites from Egyptian slavery. Samuel was called to keep the knowledge of God alive in his day. As you read the Bible, you will be able to recognize many other examples of people who were chosen to perform certain tasks.

These are examples of specific guidance for certain purposes. In the lives of many individuals, the will of God may not be spelled out in such specific detail. God seems to give His children a great deal of latitude in determining the exact shape of His will for them. The important condition is that we are always in His moral will, that is, obeying His commandments and not contradicting anything He has told us.

When we speak of doing the will of God, we generally refer to the life purpose of an individual. We may also be talking about a calling to special, full-time service.

Full-Time or Not?

It goes without saying that being a Christian is a full-time occupation. In the vocabulary of the church, however, we use the term "full-time service" to identify church-related vocations. We mean, for example, preachers, missionaries, Bible-school teachers, and evangelists who are in full-time service. They dedicate all of their time to Christian vocation and usually gain their livelihood by their ministry.

One of the first questions to ask yourself is, "Does God want me to dedicate my life to full-time service?" There are several signals to watch for in order to find the answer to this question.

First, if the Lord means for you to give your life to a ministry such as preaching or missions, He will call you to this ministry. The call comes to different people in different, but distinct, ways. A few report dramatic emotional encounters where they see visions or hear voices. This is rare, however, and usually the call is perceived as an inner impression. You begin to feel a strong desire to fulfill a certain ministry—perhaps preaching. You pray about it and ask God to make it clear, and still the feeling persists. Over a period of weeks and months, it does not wane; it intensifies. You feel you must preach or die!

"The Needs of the Congo Mission" was an article in a Christian magazine delivered by mistake to a college professor's house. He was tossing his junk mail in the wastebasket when the title of the article captured his attention. Turning to the story, these words caught his eye: "The need is great here. We have no one to work in the northern province of Gabon in the central Congo. And it is my prayer as I write this article that God will lay His hand on one—one on whom, already, the Master's eyes have been cast—that he or she shall be called to this place to help us."

The professor put the magazine aside, picked up his diary, and wrote: "My search is over!" The man's name was Albert Schweitzer, who became one of the 20th century's most well-known missionaries to Africa.

There is no specific, exact method that God uses to communicate His calling to us. We might consider Schweitzer's experience a quirk or accident, but another way of looking at it is that this was God's way of letting him know his calling. He felt inside himself that it was so.

This internal witness is generally a strong indication of God's will. Occasionally, however, it is merely a reflection of genuine admiration that the believer may have for those who occupy these ministries. There will be other indications as well.

Second, how does the church think of you? In the New Testament, the church was sometimes the agency used by the Holy Spirit to choose ministers. Acts 13:1-3 gives an interesting account of individuals identified for special Christian service by means of the church. It is generally true that if you sense an inner witness that God wishes you to serve Him in Christian vocation, your brothers and sisters in the church will confirm the calling. If they voice strong doubts, or counsel you to proceed slowly, it is a good idea to listen to their advice.

God's enablements may be thought of as a third sign of your calling. What does this mean? Simply that if God wants you to fulfill a certain ministry, He will equip you to perform it. If He wants you to become a missionary, for example, it is likely He will give you the ability to study and to learn a foreign language. He will equip you with special gifts or capabilities you will need to fulfill the ministry. God will also begin to open doors through which you may enter as you actually begin your ministry.

These three indications, then, will help you to know if the Lord wishes you to serve Him full-time: (1) You will sense an undeniable urge, or calling, within your heart; (2) the church will more than likely confirm the calling; and (3) you will recognize certain divine helps as you prepare for the fulfillment of your ministry.

God's Will for All

Only a relatively small percentage of Christians receive a calling to vocational service. The majority discover that God wishes them to serve Him in what we normally call "secular" work. This may mean that you will work as a factory employee, a nurse, a teacher, a mechanic, a waitress—or in any one of thousands of other jobs. What God expects of us all, however, is faithfulness to Him in whatever we do. He wants us to be closely related to Him so that we may be led by Him.

Jesus told a crowd of listeners, "Not everyone who says to me, 'Lord, Lord,' will enter the kingdom of heaven, but only he who does the will of my Father who is in heaven" (Matthew 7:21). A short time later He said, "For whoever does the will of my Father in heaven is my brother and sister and mother" (12:50). He seems to be saying that it is not just words that are effective in establishing a relationship with Him; rather, what interests Him most is the direction our life takes.

Walt Disney was well known by his fellow workers in film production for his willingness to cut out anything that got in the way of the advancement of the film's story. One of the *Snow White* animators, Ward Kimball, tells about working for months on drawings that resulted in a four-

and-a-half-minute sequence in which the dwarfs prepare a meal for Snow White and, in the process, fairly destroy the kitchen. It was hilarious, according to everyone who saw it. But Disney, who also laughed uproariously, cut it out of the picture because it distracted from the story's pacing.

As we think about our life story being shown as a film, is there anything there that should be eliminated in order for God to do the great things through us that He wants to perform?

In the Garden of Eden, Adam had been faced with a choice and took a selfish course, saying in effect, "I will do what I want." But Jesus, faced with a choice in the Garden of Gethsemane, said, "Not what I will, but what you [God] will" (Mark 14:35). Jesus gave us His personal example to teach us perfect submission to the Father's will.

Steps to Follow

The first step in discovering God's will is a surrendered life. Psalm 40:8 voices the sentiments of a consecrated man: "I desire to do your will, O my God; your law is within my heart." One follows the other: A man can desire God's will only when his heart is right with God.

Perhaps the best-known call for a surrendered life in all the Bible is Romans 12:1: "Therefore, I urge you, brothers, in view of God's mercy, to offer your bodies as living sacrifices, holy and pleasing to God—this is your spiritual act of worship." The result of offering yourself is explained in verse 2: "Then you will be able to test and approve what God's will is—his good, pleasing and perfect will."

The second step is prayer. Scripture records instances of people praying and seeking divine direction. Psalm 143:10 is such a petition: "Teach me to do your will, for you are my God." In Colossians 1:9, Paul offered a prayer for the people of a local church, asking God to show them His will: "For this reason, since the day we heard about you, we have not stopped praying for you and asking God to fill you with the knowledge of his will."

The third step is obedience. While God's complete plan for your whole life will not be unfolded all at once, it is certain that He will reveal some aspects of His will as you study the Bible and pray. For instance, there are some clear indications of God's will, like the following instructions:

It is God's will that you should be sanctified: that you should avoid sexual immorality; that each of you should learn to control his own body in a way that is holy and honorable (1 Thessalonians 4:3).

Be joyful always; pray continually; give thanks in all circumstances, for this is God's will for you in Christ Jesus (1 Thessalonians 5:16-18).

Jesus underlined the importance of obeying God's will by a parable He told about two sons:

"What do you think? There was a man who had two sons. He went to the first and said, 'Son, go and work today in the vineyard.'

"'I will not,' he answered, but later he changed his mind and went.

"Then the father went to the other son and said the same thing. He answered, 'I will, sir,' but he did not go.

"Which of the two did what his father wanted?"

"The first," they answered (Matthew 21:28-31).

And There Are Rewards

We must not suppose that this matter of knowing and doing God's will is the beginning of a road of suffering and affliction; quite the opposite is the case. It is true that at times the will of God may entail difficulties. The will of God for His Son led Him to a cross. For Paul it included shipwreck.

Leadership magazine tells the following story:

Joseph Ton was pastor of Second Baptist Church, Oradea, Rumania, until he was exiled by the Rumanian government in 1981. In *Pastoral Renewal*, he writes of his experience: "Years ago I ran away from my country to study theology at Oxford. In 1972, when I was ready to go back to Rumania, I discussed my plans with some fellow students. One student asked, 'Joseph, what chances do you have of successfully implementing your plans?'"

He asked God about it, and God brought to mind Matthew 10:16—"I send you forth as sheep in the midst of wolves"

[KJV]—and seemed to say, "Tell me, what chance does a sheep surrounded by wolves have of surviving five minutes, let alone of converting the wolves? Joseph, that's how I send you: totally defenseless and without a reasonable hope of success. If you are willing to go like that, go. If you are not willing to be in that position, don't go."

Ton writes: "After our return, as I preached uninhibitedly, harassment and arrests came. One day during interrogation an officer threatened to kill me. Then I said, 'Sir, your supreme weapon is killing. My supreme weapon is dying. Sir, you know my sermons are all over the country on tapes now. If you kill me, I will be sprinkling them with my blood. Whoever listens to them after that will say, *I'd better listen. This man sealed it with his blood.* They will speak ten times louder than before. So, go on and kill me. I will win the supreme victory then.'"

The officer sent him home. "That gave me pause. For years I was a Christian who was cautious because I wanted to survive. I had accepted all the restrictions the authorities put on me because I wanted to live. Now I wanted to die, and they wouldn't oblige. Now I could do whatever I wanted in Rumania. For years I wanted to save my life, and I was losing it. Now that I wanted to lose it, I was winning it" ("Living Sacrifice," Fall 1987, p. 44).

There are overwhelming rewards when you discover God's will and do it.

First, you establish a unique, intimate personal relationship with Jesus Christ. He told the people of His day, "My . . . brothers are those who hear God's word and put it into practice" (Luke 8:21).

Second, you place yourself in a position where you can learn more and more about God. You will gain a certain spiritual discernment. Jesus said, "If anyone chooses to do God's will, he will find out whether my teaching comes from God or whether I speak on my own" (John 7:17).

Finally, fulfilling the will of God in your life guarantees a right standing before God throughout eternity. Scripture lets us know: "The world and its desires pass away, but the man who does the will of God lives forever" (1 John 2:17).

To know and to do God's will is worth the necessary investment of time, energy, prayer, and consecration.

THE CHAPTER REVISITED

This chapter furnishes background about knowing and doing the will of God.

God sometimes gives specific guidance to individuals about what He wants their lives to accomplish and where He wants them to serve. Others discover that an infinite variety of possibilities opens up to them. They may choose between various directions and still be performing God's will, if they remain securely in God's moral will. Being in God's moral will means your life meets God's requirements for obeying His rules about right and wrong.

Three indispensable prerequisites for entering full-time ministry are as follows: (1) an internal drive that you sense comes from God, (2) confirmation by brothers and sisters in the church and (3) God's enablements for ministry and open doors that lead toward a need being met. Three spiritual requirements must also be met: a surrendered life, prayer, and obedience.

Understand that God may not—probably *will not*—show you everything. His Word, the psalmist wrote, is a lamp to your feet and a light to your pathway (Psalm 119:105). The lamps of Old Testament days were floating wicks in containers of oil. The light they cast was a circle, like the glow of a candle, that advanced only as the light-bearer moved forward. God's guidance is often similar. We err by wanting enough brilliance to illuminate a mile down the road; God provides sufficient light for the next step.

—8—

He Expects Me to Witness

⭐ What does the Bible say about witnessing?

⭐ What is the difference between evangelizing and witnessing?

⭐ How do I witness?

An interesting conversation has been imagined to have taken place when Christ returned to heaven after His life on earth. An angel asked Him, "Did You set up Your kingdom while You were there?"

Jesus replied, "I have begun it with a handful of followers, and I have entrusted to them the responsibility of spreading the gospel to the rest of the world."

"But what if they fail?" queried the angel.

Jesus answered, "I have no other plan."

This conversation is, of course, the result of someone's imagination; there is no record that it actually took place. But it teaches a truth: The method Jesus set up by which His message is to be spread throughout the earth is the personal witness of His followers. A key scripture is Acts 1:8.

The purpose of this lesson is to find out what the Bible says about witnessing and to learn how to share our faith with others. Each believer has the privilege and responsibility to cooperate with the Lord in spreading the good news of the gospel throughout the earth.

Louis Pasteur, discoverer of the rabies vaccine, lived in an era when thousands of people died each year after being bitten by rabid animals. Having worked for years on the vaccine, he was about to test it on himself when the panic-stricken mother of 9-year-old Joseph Meister rushed in and begged him to experiment on her son, who would die without help. Pasteur injected young Joseph for 10 days and, happily, he lived.

Years later, when asked what he wanted etched on his tombstone, Pasteur, who had accomplished much in his life, requested simply that they write: "Joseph Meister lived."

When we come to the end of life, our greatest legacy will

be those who live eternally because we shared our faith with them.

What the Bible Says

To the men whom He had called and who had committed themselves to Him, Jesus gave final instructions just before He left the earth to return to the Father. He told them: "Go and make disciples of all nations, baptizing them in the name of the Father and of the Son and of the Holy Spirit, and teaching them to obey everything I have commanded you. And surely I am with you always, to the very end of the age" (Matthew 28:19, 20).

He added pointedly, "But you will receive power when the Holy Spirit comes on you; and you will be my witnesses" (Acts 1:8).

These clear instructions to His followers came after He had already taught them that they were to share the gospel and after He had given them practical experience in witnessing. You can read about their earlier witnessing efforts in Matthew 10 and Luke 9. The account in Luke starts with this explanation: "When Jesus had called the Twelve together, he gave them power and authority to drive out all demons and to cure diseases, and he sent them out to preach the kingdom of God and to heal the sick" (Luke 9:1, 2). Jesus is still depending on His friends to tell the world about Him.

Some people might read these verses and suppose that only the 12 disciples were to be involved in representing

Christ to the world. But this is a ministry that calls for the participation of all Christians. One of the plainest statements of this truth is 2 Corinthians 5:17-20:

> Therefore, if anyone is in Christ, he is a new creation; the old has gone, the new has come! All this is from God, who reconciled us to himself through Christ and gave us the ministry of reconciliation: that God was reconciling the world to himself in Christ, not counting men's sins against them. And he has committed to us the message of reconciliation. We are therefore Christ's ambassadors, as though God were making his appeal through us. We implore you on Christ's behalf: Be reconciled to God.

This passage uses the word *ambassador*, which we still use in government language today. An ambassador is one empowered and commissioned to represent his head of government in a foreign land. We are here on earth representing our divine head, Jesus Christ, who resides in heaven. These verses make clear, too, the nature of our work as ambassadors. We are to be engaged in the work of reconciliation, which means that we try to bring men into a right relationship with God, from whom they are separated by sin.

Once you became a Christian and committed yourself to obey and serve the Lord, you became His witness.

Evangelist and Witness: What's the Difference?

An evangelist, as we normally use the word today, is one who travels from place to place preaching the gospel with the aim of making converts. This is essentially the New Testament view of the ministry of an evangelist.

A witness is somewhat different. A witness is a person who talks to another about something he has seen or experienced. You can be a witness without being an evangelist. The Christian witness and the evangelist have something in common, however: both want to make converts. The Christian witness shares what he has experienced with another because he wants that person to enjoy the same experience.

Apparently, only a relatively few people are called to be evangelists; but all of us are called to be witnesses.

How Can I Witness?

You may be like many other Christians who want to be witnesses but are not sure how to go about it. Paul Little, in his book *How to Give Away Your Faith,* shares some helpful suggestions. These are based on an encounter that Jesus had with a woman of Samaria, as told in John 4.

1. *Get to know people.* Jesus approached a public well at about the same time as did a woman from the community. He didn't avoid meeting her; as a matter of fact, He initiated a conversation.

We, too, need to make it our business to get to know unsaved people. If we don't make contacts among non-Christians, we will not make converts. Look for ways to establish friendships. While it is admirable to live a life separated from sin, it is wrong to separate yourself completely from nonbelievers.

2. *Talk about things that interest the other person.* In His interview with the Samaritan woman, Christ began their conversation by talking about water, because obviously she had come to get water from the well. We need to look for something that interests the other person so we can talk on common ground.

3. *Try to stimulate interest.* One of the best textbooks on witnessing is James Kennedy's *Evangelism Explosion.* It contains a simple outline of the gospel, which the witnessing encounter should ultimately include. Kennedy suggests the use of two questions. The first one asks, "Have you come to the place in your spiritual life where you know that if you were to die tonight, you would go to heaven?" A second question follows: "If you stood in the presence of God and He asked you, 'Why should I permit you to enter heaven?' what would you answer?" The two queries penetrate to the heart of the matter of salvation and how a person is saved.

Another method suggests the use of several leading questions about family, occupation, and religion, which stimulate interest in spiritual things and lead up to the gospel presentation.

4. *Don't rush a decision.* Sometimes, in our eagerness to get our unsaved acquaintances to make a spiritual decision, we ride roughshod over their feelings, even to the point of making ourselves unwelcome in the future.

Remember that conversion is not a human work; it is a

spiritual matter. The Holy Spirit in the One who ultimately convicts a sinner of sin and convinces him to turn to Christ. We need to discover the fine balance between presenting the gospel, with its demands and urgency, and overdoing the presentation.

5. *Be positive.* A common error in witnessing is to come down hard on the vices and bad habits of the person to whom you are testifying. We know that God condemns immorality and unclean living; consequently, there is a tendency always to crusade for reform. But remember that the call of Christ is not to quit smoking and drinking. His call is "Come to the Cross." The sanctified life follows conversion; it doesn't precede it.

Good advice, then, is not to condemn and blame, but rather always to present a message of hope. The old proverb, "You catch more flies with honey than with vinegar" can be applied directly to your witnessing attitude.

6. *Don't debate.* The Samaritan woman began to feel uncomfortable in the presence of Christ, so she endeavored to change the subject to something controversial—a religious question. Jesus deftly answered the question and came right back to the heart of her problem.

People invariably bring up foolish questions, such as, "Where did Cain get his wife?" Or they attempt to spotlight doctrinal differences among denominations in order to change the subject. This is usually because they feel uncomfortable about their own personal spiritual condition. A good rule is to try not to get sidetracked.

7. *Press for an answer.* This is the other side of number 4. While it is true that you should not try to force a person against his will, neither should you leave a neutral impression. The claims of Christ deserve and require an answer. Impress upon the person that he cannot remain forever in the valley of decision as far as Christ is concerned; in his mind and will, he must decide one way or another.

Be careful that you grasp the significance of the distinction between pressing for an answer and forcing a decision. You are not to rush the question, but you are to underline the fact that one cannot be neutral about the most important questions of eternity.

God Gets People Ready

Before Paul ever spoke the first word of faith-sharing in the city of Corinth, God assured him, "I have many people in this city" (Acts 18:10). The assurance that God was giving His servant was that He was going before the apostle and getting people ready to receive and respond to the message that he would bring. God does that. He works on the other person's heart to receive the message even before He works on you to share it.

An unusual church in Cincinnati, the Vineyard, practices a kind of servanthood that shares God's love in practical ways. Joe Delaney and his 8-year-old son, Jared, lived in the same city. The little boy once asked his father: "Is there really a God?" His dad, who had little church contact, answered honestly, "Son, I don't really know."

Jared ran inside, returned with a helium balloon and a 3x5 card on which he wrote, "God, if You're real, send people who know You to Dad and me."

Two days later, Joe and son pulled into a church-sponsored car wash and were told that it was absolutely free. "Why?" asked Joe. "Just to show people God's love in a practical way," the pastor, Steve Sjogren, responded.

"Do you people believe in God?" Jared asked.

"We sure do," the pastor answered.

From that initial contact, a relationship began that ultimately led both father and son to faith in Christ. We never know when God is getting people ready.

Witnessing Expects Results

When the Lord left instructions for us to go and to witness, it was with the expectation that there would be results.

"You did not choose me, but I chose you and appointed you to go and bear fruit—fruit that will last," He told us (John 15:16). Shortly afterward He prayed that the Father would be with all of His followers: "My prayer is not for them alone. I pray also for those who will believe in me through their message" (17:20). Jesus believed that when His followers witnessed, they would gain converts.

Closely akin to the matter of witnessing is the subject of workers for the spiritual harvest. To help us understand the nature of our task, Jesus compared the unsaved people of the world to a great field of grain that was ready to be reaped. He counseled us, "The harvest is plentiful but the workers are few. Ask the Lord of the harvest, therefore, to send out workers into his harvest field" (Matthew 9:37, 38). Part of your efforts to win people, then, will go beyond your direct personal testimony and will involve praying to the Father to send still more workers who will also try to win people.

We must witness and pray for more witnesses.

Jesus has no other plan.

THE CHAPTER REVISITED

Chapter 8 tells about sharing your faith with lost people who need to hear, understand, and receive the message of Christ's love and grace.

We miss out on the blessing of witnessing because we have the mistaken impression that we must memorize long lists of scriptures, complex formulas, or complicated theology. A witness, however, is simply a person who shares with someone else what he himself has experienced.

A good model for faith-sharing is the contact Jesus made with a woman of Samaria in John 4. This instructive Biblical passage describes a low-key, friendship approach used by Christ that resulted in this woman's conversion and her subsequent witness to many of her hometown acquaintances. Principles of this encounter are applicable to a pattern that we may follow today.

Bottom line: Each of us sharing with others what God through Christ has done in our lives is heaven's plan for earth's salvation.

FOR FURTHER STUDY

Adist, Christopher. *Personal Disciple Making.* Laguna Hills, Calif.: Here's Life Publishers.

Kennedy, D. James. *Evangelism Explosion.* Wheaton, Ill.: Tyndale House Publishers, 1983.

Little, Paul E. *How to Give Away Your Faith.* Downers Grove, Ill.: InterVarsity Press, 1988.

Strobel, Lee. *Inside the Mind of Unchurched Harry and Mary.* Grand Rapids: Zondervan, 1993.

Sustar, T. David. *Transforming Faith.* Cleveland, Tenn.: Pathway Press, 1992.

—9—

He Expects Me to Exercise Stewardship

★ What is stewardship?

★ Why is money management important in the Christian's life?

★ Why is giving important for the believer?

In ancient times, when slavery prevailed, it was common for the lord of the house to appoint a trusted slave to serve as the manager of his household. The duties of this manager were far-ranging. They included teaching and disciplining other members of the house, managing financial affairs, and generally acting on behalf of the master in business matters. A well-known Old Testament example is Joseph's position in the house of Potiphar (Genesis 39:4-6). This household administrator was called a steward. It was a great honor and a heavy responsibility to serve as a steward.

In the New Testament and in today's Christian service, every believer is a steward for the Lord Jesus Christ. As His servants, all of us must acknowledge that all we have belongs to Him; and we must manage it on His behalf. Our purpose in this lesson is to look at what the Bible has to say about our management of the resources we have. It attempts to make clear what our attitude ought to be toward money and other possessions. The key verse is 1 Corinthians 4:2.

Stewards From the Beginning

A part of God's original plan for man was for him to manage what God had given him. In Creation, God placed man in the midst of all that had been made and told him to rule over it. Indeed, man was to rule over everything but himself (Genesis 1—3).

Stewardship, according to Scripture, entails a great deal more than just the management of money—although how one manages money is probably the most readily observable aspect of stewardship. The apostle Peter captured the broader meaning of stewardship when he wrote: "Each one should use whatever gift he has received to serve others, faithfully administering God's grace in its various forms" (1 Peter 4:10). Paul was also talking about more than money when he observed: "Now it is required that those who have been given a trust must prove faithful" (1 Corinthians 4:2).

From earliest times, money management has figured in the relationship man has enjoyed with God. Long before Moses gave the people the Law he received from God, some men had begun the practice of dedicating a tenth of their income in worship. Abraham began the tithe (*tithe* literally means "the tenth part"). Jacob confirmed the practice, and the Law established it. "The tithe . . . is the Lord's" (Leviticus 27:30, KJV). Giving up material possessions seems always to have been a mark of reverence and devotion to God.

A business executive who traveled extensively hired a woman with a doctorate in horticulture to design a garden around his newly built estate. He told her pointedly, "I want a garden that doesn't require any maintenance. Make everything automatic."

She responded with frankness: "One thing you need to deal with. Without a gardener, there's no garden."

It's that way with taking care of what God has given you. Stewardship requires careful thought and attention.

The Bible Gives Direction

Throughout the Old Testament, men continued to bring the tithe to God, both before the giving of the Mosaic Law and afterward. The closing page of the Old Testament contains a succinct, easily understood order and promise from

God to His people: "'Bring the whole tithe into the storehouse, that there may be food in my house. Test me in this,' says the Lord Almighty, 'and see if I will not throw open the floodgates of heaven and pour out so much blessing that you will not have room enough for it'" (Malachi 3:10).

The practice of tithing continued in the time of Christ and was sanctioned by Him. He openly objected to some religious traditions of the Pharisees; but when He mentioned their custom of exercising great care that their tithe not be neglected, He said, "You are right . . . you should have done this; but you should not have neglected weightier matters like justice, mercy, and faithfulness" (Matthew 23:23, paraphrased).

Systematic, regular, percentage-related giving was taught by Paul to the members of churches which he established. He urged each Christian to set aside a sum of money on the first day of each week according to his income (1 Corinthians 16:2).

A pastor uses this illustration to teach the dynamics of tithing. He offers a man sitting in the church a $100 bill, with one proviso: "I'll give you this $100, if you will give me $10 back." No one has ever refused his offer. He is letting his people know, "God gives you all that you have, in the sense that He makes it possible for you to earn it. All He asks in return is 10 percent." Faithful tithers almost always testify that the 90 percent goes farther when they return the 10 percent to God.

Guidelines for Giving

By reading the New Testament stories of Jesus and His teachings about material possessions, we can learn a great deal about what our attitude and manner of giving should be.

While ministering on earth, Jesus was interested in how people gave to God. In Mark 12:41 we read: "Jesus sat down opposite the place where the offerings were put and watched the crowd putting their money into the temple treasury." He demonstrated genuine interest in the relative amounts that people gave. This Biblical passage is the one where Jesus commended a widow who gave a tiny offering, because the offering constituted all she had.

Two truths stand out in this account:

1. Jesus takes note of what we give.

2. The measure of an offering is not how much we give, but rather how much we have left after we have given. Jesus pointed out, "They all gave out of their wealth; but she, out of her poverty, put in everything—all she had to live on" (v. 44).

The Lord is also concerned about the heart attitude with which you give. In our day, as in His, some people give just to get a pat on the back. He talked about seeing men actually announce their offerings and gifts to the needy with trumpet blasts! They do it, He explained, "to be honored by men. . . . But when you give to the needy, do not let your left hand know what your right hand is doing, so that your giving may be in secret" (Matthew 6:2, 3). He concluded by promising that "your Father, who sees what is done in secret, will reward you [openly]" (v. 4).

The matter of rewards for giving is also prominent in the Bible. Paul counseled Christians: "Remember this: Whoever sows sparingly will also reap sparingly, and whoever sows generously will also reap generously" (2 Corinthians 9:6). Jesus himself emphasized this same point when He urged liberal giving in Luke 6:38: "Give, and it will be given to you. A good measure, pressed down, shaken together and running over, will be poured into your lap. For with the measure you use, it will be measured to you."

Giving is also noted by the Father. When Cornelius received an angelic visitor who told him to send for Simon Peter, the angel informed him, "Your prayers and gifts to the poor have come up as a memorial offering before God" (Acts 10:4). He and his whole household were subsequently saved and filled with the Spirit as a result of his faithfulness and obedience to God.

A wealthy businessman visiting the docks was irritated to see a fisherman sitting lazily beside his boat. He asked, "Why aren't you still fishing?"

"I've caught enough fish for the day," the fisherman answered.

"But why don't you go catch more fish?" the businessman challenged.

"Why would I want to do that?" the fisherman asked, to which the tycoon impatiently replied, "So you could sell them, use the money to buy a bigger boat and better nets and catch still more fish! Soon you would be rich like me."

"What would I do then?" the laid-back fisherman asked.

"Well, you could sit down and enjoy life."

"And what do you think I'm doing now?" the fisherman said.

Why Is Giving So Important?

One pastor who has outlined a plan that will allow him to preach through the Bible over a period of 20 years has announced to his congregation that they can expect to hear six years of preaching about stewardship. The Bible dedicates a great deal of space to the subject. Why? Probably because the management of possessions may be one of the best public testimonies of what really is inside the heart.

A number of parables and true stories teach us negative aspects of the money questions. Jesus taught a lesson about the Rich Fool—called this because he gave a great deal of attention to money and possessions and completely ignored the spiritual side of his life. Acts 5 recounts the death of Ananias and Sapphira, a married couple in the Jerusalem church, who lied to the leaders of the congregation about a money matter. In 1 Timothy 6:10 there is a stern warning about attaching undue affection to worldly possessions: "For the love of money is a root of all kinds of evil. Some people, eager for money, have wandered from the faith and pierced themselves with many griefs." Dozens of exhortations in the New Testament concern the proper attitude toward the proper management of money.

One of the best-known of the Lord's parables concerns the Good Samaritan. He is so named because he invested his time and money in a poor, hurt traveler who desperately needed assistance (Luke 10:25-37).

The parables of the hidden treasure and the pearl of great price (Matthew 13:44-46) teach us about proper values. The parable of the ten talents (Matthew 25:14-30) teaches accountability. The story of the unjust steward (Luke 16:1-10) teaches trustworthiness. The list could continue. Jesus taught that you can recognize a tree by the fruit it bears. In the same way, you announce to the world—and to God—a great deal about yourself by the way you exercise stewardship.

THE CHAPTER REVISITED

A Christian view of material things is that we possess nothing ourselves. We serve rather as stewards (managers) of the resources of our lives. Knowing how to manage rightly is what we call Christian stewardship.

Throughout the Old Testament and into the New, the tithe (one-tenth) was the normal expectation of people of God who desired to worship God with material possessions. Tithing was practiced before the Law was given, it was established in the Law, it was observed throughout Old Testament history, and it was sanctioned by Christ. Paul, too, taught regular, systematic giving.

Why is money management important in the Christian life? Probably because it is one of the best indications of what is really inside the heart. The New Testament recounts many parables, stories, and actual incidents that teach lessons of compassion, trustworthiness, and accountability with regard to money.

FOR FURTHER STUDY

Burkett, Larry. *How to Manage Your Money.* Chicago: Moody Press, 1993.

Ronsvale, Sylvia. *Behind Stained Glass Windows.* Grand Rapids: Baker Books, 1996.

Taylor, Al. *Proving God.* Cleveland, Tenn.: Pathway Press, 1991.

– 10 –

He Expects Me to Be a Part
of His Church

☆ What is the church?

☆ What is its nature, its purpose, and its mission?

☆ What are the duties and privileges of its members?

God has always had a people. From the dawn of time He has chosen people to be His own possession, and He has called individuals into this fellowship. The patriarchs of Genesis, the nation of Israel throughout the Old Testament, and the Christian church of the New Testament—all of these have, at various times, represented God to the world.

In this chapter we will take a Scriptural look at what it means to be the people of God in our day. We will seek the answers to these questions from the Bible. Key words you will learn about are . . .

- Exaltation

- Evangelism

- Education

- Edification

- Church

Approach this study with prayer. If it is true that the church is the only institution founded by Jesus Christ, then it certainly merits our prayerful consideration and participation. If we accept the Biblical truth that He is the Head and the church is the body, then we need to understand how the body should function. If we glory in the knowledge that He is the Bridegroom and the church is the bride, we should gladly anticipate the coming marriage in the heavens.

Our purpose in this chapter is to find out what it means to truly be the people of God.

What Is the Church?

The word *church* appears in the New Testament a little more than 100 times. Its origin is a Greek word that can be literally translated "called-out ones." It refers to a group of people who have been assembled for a particular purpose.

This is the designation chosen by Jesus himself for His people. In Matthew 16:18, He announced: "I will build my church, and the gates of Hades [hell] will not overcome [prove stronger than] it."

Theologians have written long, involved definitions of what the church is, but the following statement sums up the most important aspects: *The church is a group of redeemed people banded together for worship, study, fellowship, and evangelism.* Two other words are sometimes used to further define the church—*universal* and *local.* The *universal church* refers to all people who have been redeemed through history, those who will constitute the citizenry of heaven without regard to the branch of the church they belonged to on earth. The *local church* refers to a group of Christians gathered together in a particular place. Both ideas of the church appear in the New Testament, although about 90 percent of the references are to local churches.

The church has a special relationship with the Father. It is called God's building, His household, His temple, His people, and His city. It has special relationship with the Son, for it is called His bride, His body, His branches, and His flock. He called it "my church." The church also has a special relationship with the Holy Spirit because He constitutes the church, He empowers it, and He guides its leaders and members.

What Is the Church For?

Briefly expressed, the church exists to perform Christ's work in the world.

The Scriptures teach a number of different functions of the church, but most all of them fit in one of the following four categories.

1. *Worship.* God desires His people to worship Him. One of the most beautiful scenes of heaven, depicted in the Book of Revelation, shows a worshiping multitude before the presence of God. They sing, "You are worthy, our Lord and God, to receive glory and honor and power" (4:11). A little later an unnumbered host of angels sing, "Worthy is the Lamb, who was slain, to receive power and wealth and wisdom and strength and honor and glory and praise!" (5:12).

The church brings God's people together for corporate worship, in which brothers and sisters join their voices in prayer and song to God.

2. *Evangelism.* The church is the center of soulwinning activity. The Book of Acts serves as a brief history of the first 30 years of the church. The picture that emerges, and which can serve as a pattern for our day, is a church that was unashamedly evangelistic in outreach.

Acts 11 describes the evangelistic efforts of the church at Antioch. Involving Barnabas and Paul, the church at Antioch attempted to reach all their surrounding area. Not content with just local evangelistic efforts, the church later sent Barnabas and Paul to foreign countries to win converts and to establish churches.

A later description of the evangelistic efforts of the church at Ephesus claims, "This went on for two years, so that all the Jews and Greeks who lived in the province of Asia heard the word of the Lord" (Acts 19:10).

A typical church in New Testament times encouraged its members to reach out into nearby communities and preach, win converts, and plant churches. The new church would repeat the pattern, reaching local people and pushing out to a new community. Thus, they grew.

God's plan for His church today is that, by all means, we should win lost men and women, boys and girls.

3. *Education.* In an earlier lesson we learned that the Lord left His church some definite instructions, which we call the Great Commission, found in Matthew 28:18-20. Pulling the command verbs out of verses 19 and 20, we come up with the words "Go . . . make disciples . . . baptizing . . . teaching." In Greek, all of these verbs are in what we call participle form, except for the one that says "make disciples." Therefore, the verbs can literally read, "Going, baptizing, teaching— make disciples." "Make disciples" is the heart of the marching orders.

A disciple is one who follows another in order to learn from him. Christ's followers were called disciples. He still calls us to come to Him in order to learn. "Take my yoke upon you and learn from me," He invites us in Matthew 11:29.

The church functions to help its members learn spiritual truths. Through its agencies, such as Sunday school and midweek Bible training, the church guides us through organized programs of study that encompass all of the Bible and cover all areas of Christian living.

4. *Fellowship.* There is strength in unity. A poetic passage in the Old Testament expresses it this way: "Two are better than one, because they have a good return for their work: If one falls down, his friend can help him up. But pity the man who falls and has no one to help him up! . . . Though one may be overpowered, two can defend themselves. A cord of three strands is not quickly broken" (Ecclesiastes 4:9-12).

The New Testament church is characterized by unity and fellowship: "They devoted themselves to the apostles' teaching and to the fellowship, to the breaking of bread and to prayer. . . . Every day they continued to meet together in the temple courts. They broke bread in their homes and ate together with glad and sincere hearts, praising God and enjoying the favor of all the people" (Acts 2:42, 46, 47). This kind of quality time spent together with the people of God is a foretaste of the unity that heaven promises.

Lee Iacocca, the former Chrysler chief executive officer (CEO), asked Vince Lombardi, the great football coach, the secret of an outstanding football team. Lombardi's answer appears in the book *Iacocca*:

There are a lot of coaches with good ball clubs who know the fundamentals and have plenty of discipline but still don't win the game. Then you come to the third ingredient: if you're going to play together as a team, you've got to care for one another. You've got to *love* each other. Each player has to be thinking about the next guy and saying to himself: "If I don't block that man, Paul is going to get his legs broken. I have to do my job well in order that he can do his." The difference between mediocrity and greatness is the feeling these guys have for each other (David Abodaher, *Iacocca*, New York: MacMillan, 1982).

He could have been describing the church!

These four aspects of the church's activity—worship, evangelism, education, and fellowship—encompass the purposes of the church.

Is the Church Perfect?

A young man experienced a dramatic conversion and immediately joined the church, basking in the afterglow of his encounter with Christ. He avidly studied the Bible and enjoyed the company of his new brothers. To his great surprise, he soon discovered that among the church membership were two families who would not even speak to each other because of some minor disagreement that had surfaced a year or so before. Disheartened, he complained to his pastor, "You would think that children of God could get along together!"

The wise pastor took the youngster to Acts 6, which

describes one of the first church squabbles. "These people lived in the shadow of the Cross and could still hear the echo from the Upper Room," he said, "and yet we recognize that they had problems among themselves." The good thing is that these problems can be resolved by praying, concerned people.

The Bible teaches the doctrine of glorification, which means that at some time in the future—at the coming of the Lord—we will be changed and made like our Lord. Until then, however, church members are human and will likely err. Our humanity is not an excuse for sin; in fact, the Bible says that we are not to sin (1 John 2:1). However, New Testament examples of quarreling, lying, envying, strife, and divisions within the church provide sufficient evidence to let us know that the church will probably experience internal difficulties until Jesus comes. It is our responsibility to pray and seek for spiritual answers to temporal problems and to follow the leadership that God has entrusted to gifted men. These men, God tells us in Acts 20:28, have been made overseers and shepherds of the church of God by the Holy Spirit.

The Church and Its Government

The church is made up of local congregations who, together, form a worldwide fellowship. In the Church of God the officers include pastors and overseers who coordinate the work of the church on district, state or territorial, and international levels.

The doctrines and teachings of the church are expressed

in the Declaration of Faith and in a list of teachings and practices taken from the Bible. When believers become members of the church, they hear these statements read and promise to live by them.

The church celebrates three ordinances taught by Scripture: Water Baptism, the Lord's Supper, and Footwashing.

God's View of the Church

God has expressed a high opinion of His church. He inspired Peter to write: "But you are a chosen people, a royal priesthood, a holy nation, a people belonging to God, that you may declare the praises of him who called you out of darkness into his wonderful light. Once you were not a people, but now you are the people of God" (1 Peter 2:9, 10).

God sees the church as a victorious union. Some men and women throughout history have been quick and ready to discount the church. They have predicted its decease and demise. But it still lives. It is alive and well. Born in a blaze of Pentecostal fire, it survives intact and powerful today—20 centuries later. The church is always, however, only one generation from extinction. Consequently, we must carefully study what the Bible says about the church, then prayerfully and sincerely commit ourselves to upholding its purposes and its doctrines.

When Jesus comes back, He is coming for His church.

THE CHAPTER REVISITED

During His time on earth, Jesus established only one institution—the church. Since He brought it into being and gave its marching orders, we can't be cavalier or adopt a take-it-or-leave-it attitude toward the church. If it is true that He is the head of the church and we are part of the body that He heads, then we need to know where we fit in.

The church is made up of "called-out ones," the genuinely converted. The mission of the church is fourfold: worship, evangelism, education, and fellowship. You might remember these purposes with four *E*'s: exaltation, evangelism, education, and edification.

The church is not made up of perfect people. God has entrusted its leadership to gifted men, however, and with the guidance of the Holy Spirit its troubles can be resolved. God has expressed an exalted opinion of the church. We, then, need to think of it just as highly as God does.

FOR FURTHER STUDY

Chapman, Mike. *Church Membership.* Cleveland, Tenn.: Pathway Press, 1994.

Colkmire, Lance. *Welcome to the Family.* Cleveland, Tenn.: Pathway Press, 1994.

George, Bill. *Added to the Church.* Cleveland, Tenn.: Pathway Press, 1987.

–11–

He Expects Me to Use
My Spiritual Gifts

☆ What are spiritual gifts?

☆ Who receives spiritual gifts?

☆ How many gifts are there?

How can a Christian discover, develop, and employ his gifts?

Every Christian has been endowed by his Lord with certain abilities which enable him to serve God and mankind better. We call these endowments "spiritual gifts." They are spiritual because they are of divine origin. They are gifts in that they are freely bestowed.

Like most Christians, you may ponder at times the great

task which confronts the church and wonder how we, as weak human beings, can possibly hope to accomplish the work we have been given. The answer is found in the recognition that the same Lord who has charged the church to win and to teach the world has also equipped its members to perform the mission. This equipment comes in the form of spiritual gifts.

The purpose of this chapter is to learn about spiritual gifts, how to develop them, and how to use them.

What Are Spiritual Gifts?

"Now about spiritual gifts, brothers, I do not want you to be ignorant," wrote the apostle Paul in 1 Corinthians 12:1. Despite his expressed desire, and the full explanation of spiritual gifts which he wrote in the following three chapters, the Christian world is still woefully lacking in knowledge about spiritual gifts.

Why is this? Some of the gifts that are mentioned in Paul's treatise were commonly recognized and employed in the early church. They are not accepted in many Christian circles today, however. Because such practices as speaking in tongues, interpretation of tongues, and the working of miracles are mentioned in the catalog of gifts, the whole subject has generally been ignored by the contemporary church until recently.

A Scriptural study of the matter reveals that God has indeed made provision for each believer to utilize in his life special abilities that enable him to fulfill his call to service in the Kingdom. The word *ability* indicates capacity to do effective work. It suggests the idea that the Christian, by reason of his gifts, is qualified and strengthened to satisfy the responsibilities that God has given him.

Who Has Spiritual Gifts?

The teaching of the New Testament is that every one of us has received a gift or gifts. The following Scripture passages support this claim:

- "But to each one of us grace has been given as Christ apportioned it. This is why it says: 'When he ascended on high, he led captives in his train and gave gifts to men'" (Ephesians 4:7, 8).

- "Now to each one the manifestation of the Spirit is given for the common good. . . . All these are the work of one and the same Spirit, and he gives them to each one, just as he determines" (1 Corinthians 12:7, 11).

- "Just as each of us has one body with many members, and these members do not all have the same function, so in Christ we who are many form one body, and each member belongs to all the others. We have different gifts, according to the grace given us" (Romans 12:4-6).

- "Each one should use whatever gift he has received to serve others, faithfully administering God's grace in its various forms" (1 Peter 4:10).

These and other verses make it clear that the gifts are not reserved for favored people with above-average natural abilities; they are for all.

How Many Gifts Are There?

Many good books about spiritual gifts have been produced by Christian authors. An interesting phenomenon is that these books suggest a wide variety in the number of gifts which the Bible indicates are available. Some suggest that certain gifts ceased a few decades after Christ first gave them (an idea unsupported by the Bible). Some count nine gifts; others count 18, 19, 27, or 30. There are repetitions in the lists given in the New Testament. Although gifts are mentioned in various passages, there are five principal lists.

Romans 12:6-8

Prophesying	Giving
Serving (ministry)	Governing (leadership)
Teaching	Showing mercy
Encouraging	
(exhorting)	

1 Corinthians 12:6-10

Word of wisdom	Prophecy
Word of knowledge	Discerning of spirits

Faith   Different kinds of tongues

Healings   Interpretation of tongues

Working of miracles

1 Corinthians 12:28

Apostles   Those who have gifts of healing

Prophets   Those who help others

Teachers   Those with gifts of administration

Workers of miracles   Those speaking in different kinds of tongues

Ephesians 4:11

Apostles   Evangelists

Prophets   Pastors and teachers

1 Peter 4:11

Speaking   Serving (ministering)

These lists contain duplications and perhaps overlap. They do not include other gifts which are mentioned in other settings or demonstrated by other examples—such as the gift of celibacy, missionary, and hospitality, to name a few. Some Christians believe the Scriptural designations are general and that there may be room for other specific gifts besides those named. However, they suggest that any God-given endowment which equips a person for service and that edifies the body of Christ might be considered a spiritual gift.

Is there a distinction between "spiritual gifts" and "natural talents"? An essential difference seems to be that anyone—Christian or not—may possess talents. Talents, generally, are apparent in the unconverted as well as the converted, and they are not necessarily used for spiritual edification. For example, some outstanding college professors who can captivate their audiences as they teach are men and women who are far from God. Their ability is a talent for teaching.

On the other hand, a spiritual gift seems to date from conversion. It is given for spiritual service and it is exercised to serve and to edify others.

How Can I Discover My Gift?

You can do several things that will help you to find out what spiritual gift God has given you. You can also learn how to use your gift to benefit the kingdom of God and to bring glory to the Giver.

1. *Pray.* "Do not be anxious about anything, but in everything, by prayer and petition, with thanksgiving, present your requests to God" (Philippians 4:6). This counsel from Paul tells us that we are not to worry about discovering our

spiritual gifts; rather, we are to ask God to show us. "We have not, because we ask not" is as true today as when James wrote it 2,000 years ago (see James 4:2, KJV).

2. *Study the possibilities.* Read the passages in the Bible which discuss spiritual gifts, considering the various gifts together with your own personality, desires, and feelings. Realize that two or more gifts frequently seem to be combined in the lives of individuals. For example, a man may have the gift of teaching and, at the same time, also have the gift of encouragement. (Barnabas seems to be an example of this gift combination.)

3. *Act on faith.* Once you have made the question of your gift a matter of prayer, act on the impressions you receive. It is certain that if God has equipped you to serve Him, He will not wish to keep it a secret from you! This then is a suggestion: If you believe you may have the gift of teaching, try teaching. (Understand, however, that not all gifts are subject to this kind of experimentation.)

4. *Obey the Spirit.* The Holy Spirit distributes the various gifts according to the grace of God. In explaining how the members of the church work together to accomplish the desired purpose, the Bible compares the church to a human body, each part serving its particular function. In 1 Corinthians 12:18, Paul makes it clear that "God has arranged the parts in the body, every one of them, just as he wanted them to be."

If God, by His Spirit, has dispensed gifts throughout the church, He will allow His Spirit to lead each one to the proper exercise of His gift.

A Word of Caution

It is possible for a Christian to go through life without using his spiritual gift. Certainly, this is displeasing to God; and when we stand before the judgment seat of Christ, we will have to answer for our failure to obey in this respect (see 1 Corinthians 3:10-15; 2 Corinthians 5:10).

Gifts may also be abused. Timothy was warned about neglecting his gift (1 Timothy 4:14); he was also told to "stir up" his gift (2 Timothy 1:6, KJV).

What Christ desires above all else in the stewardship of spiritual gifts is faithfulness. This is illustrated nowhere more clearly than in the parable of the talents (Matthew 25:14-30). "To one he gave five talents of money, to another two talents, and to another one talent, each according to his ability. . . . After a long time the master of those servants returned and settled accounts with them" (vv. 15, 19).

How tremendous it will be when one day we stand before the Master and hear Him say, "Well done, good and faithful servant!" (v. 21).

THE CHAPTER REVISITED

This chapter on spiritual gifts deals with a doctrine that has been largely neglected until recent years. The rediscovery of spiritual gifts parallels the rise and spread of the Pentecostal and Charismatic movements during the 20th century.

Spiritual gifts are special enablements given by the Spirit to each believer, to help him or her fulfill a calling in the context of the church. According to an abundance of Scriptural evidence, spiritual gifts are not restricted to a few special people; rather, they are distributed by the Spirit throughout the body of Christ. They differ from natural talents in significant ways.

The major passages on spiritual gifts in the Bible do not, apparently, exhaust the possibilities for giftedness; there is no single, clear, concise listing of all the gifts. The names of the gifts seem to overlap. A believer can seek to discover and develop his spiritual gifts by praying, studying the possibilities, acting on faith, and obeying the promptings of the Holy Spirit.

It is possible to err concerning spiritual gifts in two directions: ignoring the matter of spiritual gifts and abusing them. Faithful Christians will want to discover, develop, and use their giftedness!

FOR FURTHER STUDY

Chapman, Mike. *Developing Your Spiritual Gifts.* Cleveland, Tenn.: Church of God Lay Ministries, 1993.

Sustar, T. David. *A Layman's Guide to the Fruit of the Spirit.* Cleveland, Tenn.: Pathway Press, 1990.

Wagner, C. Peter. *Your Spiritual Gifts Can Help Your Church Grow.* Glendale, Calif.: Regal Books, 1994.

–12–

He Expects Me to Expect Him

 Why will Jesus come back?

 How will He come back?

 What happens then?

You, as a Christian, are heir to what the Bible calls "the blessed hope." This "hope" refers to the doctrine of the Second Coming of Christ. Consider these four contrasts:

1. Jesus came the first time as a baby; He is coming again as a conquering King.

2. He came the first time as the child of peasant parents, cradled in a barn; He will come again accompanied by "tens of thousands" of victory-winning saints.

3. He came the first time to the lullaby of angels; He will come the second time with a shout and a trumpet blast.

4. He came the first time in humiliation; He will come again in exaltation and glory.

The return of Christ signals the consummation of history as we know it. It will be the reality for which Christians have long waited, prayed, and hoped. This hope is one of the strongest incentives to live a holy life and to always seek to perform God's will. For these reasons, this final chapter is dedicated to a study of the coming of Christ.

Its purpose is to lead us into discovering more about Christ's second coming so that we can be prepared for it and tell others about it. A key Scriptural passage for this pivotal doctrine is 1 Thessalonians 4:13-18.

What We Already Have

God has made rich provisions for His people. Someone has counted more than 30,000 promises in the Bible. When we add up the statements of blessing that we have been assured of, it is almost unbelievable. Despite the fact that we are subject to difficulties, temptations, accidents, and sickness, the advantages of being a Christian, even if measured only in terms of this life, easily outweigh whatever disadvantages someone may claim.

- We have peace with God.

- We have the satisfaction of knowing that our sin has been covered and our guilt taken away.

- We have the assurance of forgiveness.

- We have received the Holy Spirit.

- We can live in harmony with others.

- Our needs are being supplied.

- We can boldly approach the Father to request healing when sickness comes.

- We know that we will be given divine direction.

Promise mounts upon promise to prove to the world that we are of all people most blessed. It is no wonder that words like *joy, peace, love, happiness,* and so forth, are frequently heard in the vocabulary of the Christian.

But this is not all. Paul stated it rather bluntly when he wrote: "If only for this life we have hope in Christ, we are to be pitied more than all men" (1 Corinthians 15:19). Thank God, there is more. Everything in Scripture points to it and everything within us cries out for it. *God is not finished with us in this life.* The ultimate revelation of God to His people will be when Jesus comes back to earth.

He Promised He Would Come

Jesus frequently told His disciples that He would come again. In one of His last discussions with them, He told them pointedly that He was going away to the Father's house to prepare a place for them. "And if I go and prepare a place for you, I will come back and take you to be with me that you also may be where I am," He promised (John 14:3).

Someone has counted more than 300 references to the Second Coming in the pages of the New Testament. These teachings fall most often from the lips of Jesus himself, but it is a doctrine common to all the writers. Paul frequently mentioned and explored the theme. It was prominent in the sermons preached by the apostles, including Peter. According to Acts 1:11, angels renewed the promise that Jesus had already made to the disciples. Jude predicted it. John anticipated it.

He Tells Why He Will Come

In the last chapter of the Bible, where the promise to return is repeated three times, Jesus indicates part of the purpose for His coming back: "Behold, I am coming soon! My reward is with me, and I will give to everyone according to what he has done. I am the Alpha and the Omega, the First and the Last, the Beginning and the End" (Revelation 22:12, 13). Capsuled in these verses are definitive reasons why He will return. At the heart of the matter is the fact that He will reward His people.

If your experience has been typical, you have encountered people who doubt the gospel. There are some who believe that the content of the Bible has been fabricated by men. To the multitudes who openly believe this—and to many others who live as if they believe it—Jesus' coming will be the final proof of the truth of God's revelation. When Jesus says that He is the Alpha and Omega, He literally means that in Him dwells the completeness of God's making Himself known. (Alpha and omega are the first and last letters of the Greek alphabet; they are like A and Z in the English language.) According to John 1:1-3, Jesus was in the beginning, and all things were made by Him; He will also be at the ending when all things will be climaxed by Him.

His coming will show the world that the Bible is true, that good ultimately overcomes evil, and that there is moral order in the universe God created.

The matter of rewards is further explained in other passages, such as 1 Corinthians 3:10-15. You, as a redeemed child of the Father, will not be subjected to the same judgment as non-Christians; however, each believer will have his life and work scrutinized and will receive a recompense based on the quality of his life and service. The inconveniences and sufferings that may be your lot here on earth will be quickly forgotten. Paul writes, "For our light and momentary troubles are achieving for us an eternal glory that far outweighs them all" (2 Corinthians 4:17).

The zenith of our reward will be the truth of 1 John 3:2, 3: "Dear friends, now we are children of God, and what we will be has not yet been made known. But we know that when he appears, we shall be like him, for we shall see him as he is."

He Tells How He Will Come

Beginning readers of the Bible are sometimes puzzled by two seemingly contradictory statements that predict the coming of Christ. First Thessalonians 5:2 says He will come as a thief in the night, while Matthew 24:27 indicates that His coming will be like lightning that flashes across the sky. How can you reconcile these two opposite statements?

Other Biblical passages shed light on the matter. The message of 1 Thessalonians 4:13-18 is one of the best explanations of Christ's coming as a thief in the night:

> Brothers, we do not want you to be ignorant about those who fall asleep, or to grieve like the rest of men, who have no hope. We believe that Jesus died and rose again and so we believe that God will bring with Jesus those who have fallen asleep in him. According to the Lord's own word, we tell you that we who are still alive, who are left till the coming of the Lord, will certainly not precede those who have fallen asleep. For the Lord himself will come down from heaven, with a loud command, with the voice of the archangel and with the trumpet call of God, and the dead in Christ will rise first. After that, we who are still alive and are left will be caught up together with them in the clouds to meet the Lord in the air. And so we will be with the Lord forever. Therefore encourage each other with these words.

His coming will be like the coming of a thief only in that it will be totally unexpected and will occur suddenly. It will take the world by surprise. The event described here is sometimes called the Rapture, a word which captures the idea expressed by the phrase "caught up" in verse 17. Christ will appear in the air and will draw to Himself all Christians who have ever lived or who are now alive.

The "caught up" Christian will meet the Lord and return to heaven with Him. After a period of celebration and peace in His presence, Christ will return, this time all the way to the earth. With an army at His side, He will defeat—for time and eternity—the Evil One. This activity of His coming is like the lightning, for all the world will see it.

What Happens Then?

We have never seen the world like God made it and as He intended it to be. Our world is under a curse of sin which settled over it when man rebelled against God's lordship. This curse has affected all of nature.

Christ's second coming initiates a new world order. We can look beyond His coming to the final triumph that it makes possible. Peace, which has for centuries eluded the desires and efforts of good men, is achieved. A blessed world ministers to its inhabitants. The gates of the city of God are opened and access to the Tree of Life is granted.

The closing pages of the Bible paint a beautiful picture. We will hunger or thirst no more. There will be no tears. His servants shall see His face.

Peter realized the tremendous spiritual value that the knowledge of the Second Coming would be to each Christian:

"Since everything will be destroyed in this way, what kind of people ought you to be? You ought to live holy and godly lives as you look forward to the day of God and speed its coming" (2 Peter 3:11, 12).

Writing in a similar vein, Paul counsels:

For the grace of God that brings salvation has appeared to all men. It teaches us to say "No" to ungodliness and worldly passions, and to live self-controlled, upright and godly lives in this present age, while we wait for the blessed hope—the glorious appearing of our great God and Savior, Jesus Christ, who gave himself for us to redeem us from all wickedness and to purify for himself a people that are his very own, eager to do what is good (Titus 2:11-14).

His coming—it is your blessed hope!

So What?

Alfred Nobel, Swedish inventor of dynamite and other powerful explosives, was surprised to read the newspaper one morning and discover his obituary written there. Actually, it was Alfred's older brother who had died and the newspaper reporter had gotten the facts wrong.

Here's something of what the obituary contained: "Alfred Nobel, the inventor of dynamite, who died yesterday, devised a way for more people to be killed in a war than ever before, and he died a very rich man."

Shaken, the inventor realized that people would remember him just as the reporter had written about him, unless he did something about it. What Nobel did was establish the Nobel Prize, the reward for scientists, inventors, writers, and others who promote peace. Recalling the chain of events later, he wrote, "Every man ought to have the chance to correct his epitaph in midstream and write a new one."

Thinking about the reality of the Second Coming will do the same thing for us.

He is coming back!

THE CHAPTER REVISITED

Jesus Christ came into the world the first time some 2,000 years ago. "He came to that which was his own, but his own did not receive him" (John 1:11) is the commentary of Scripture on that first coming. He is coming again and every eye shall see Him and every knee shall bow before His lordship. Christians eagerly await the Second Coming.

Jesus himself affirmed the truth of His coming again, as did His apostles. More than 300 times in the New Testament, the truth of the Second Coming is established. The purpose of His coming is to bring closure to history as we know it, as well as to bring rewards and blessings to His people.

Initial readings about the Second Coming seem to lead to contradictory conclusions. A careful study, however, indicates that first He comes to receive His people into His presence; then He comes to bring judgment to a world that has rejected Him.

The blessings of His second coming cause Christians to cry out in the closing words of the Book of Revelation, "Even so, come, Lord Jesus!"

FOR FURTHER STUDY

Britt, George. *When Dust Shall Sing.* Cleveland, Tenn.: Pathway Press, 1985.

Buxton, Clyne W. *End Times.* Cleveland, Tenn.: Pathway Press, 1993.